Finding Meaning in Narnia: A Voyage on the Dawn Treader

Gina Burkart, EdD

Nimble Books LLC

Nimble Books LLC
1521 Martha Avenue
Ann Arbor, MI, USA 48103
http://www.NimbleBooks.com
wfz@nimblebooks.com
+1.734-330-2593

Copyright 2011 by Gina Burkart

Version 1.0; last saved 2010-12-27.

Printed in the United States of America

ISBN-13: 978-1-60888-098-0

∞ The paper used in this publication meets the minimum requirements of the American National Standard for Information Sciences—Permanence of Paper for Printed Library Materials, ANSI Z39.48-1992. The paper is acid-free and lignin-free.

DEDICATION

For my Godchild, Ashley—who is wise beyond her years.

For my daughter, Brie—a model of self-discipline, endurance, and hard work.

For my son, Adam—the bravest young man I know.

For my youngest, Emma—a compassionate servant of others and ambassador of kindness.

INTRODUCTION

While I focused on the theological virtues of Faith, Hope, and Love in *Finding Purpose in Narnia: A Journey with Prince Caspian*, here I offer the cardinal virtues of prudence, temperance, courage, and justice as a means for reflecting on and discussing *The Dawn Treader*. Together, the theological virtues and the cardinal virtues form the seven virtues known as the seven heavenly virtues. And as faith serves as the guiding virtue of the three theological virtues, here, you will find that prudence serves as the umbrella of the four cardinal virtues.

As you find these four virtues in the following four sections, you will see how these virtues are illustrated in Lewis's characters in his book *The Voyage of the Dawn Treader*. Additionally, I offer examples of how Lewis struggled with and grew in these virtues in his life and how we might use Scripture and Lewis's book to grow in these virtues in our own lives. Real life examples are offered to demonstrate how these virtues that come from Scripture and were discussed by the Greek philosophers Socrates and Plato and the Christian theologian St. Thomas Aquinas are still relevant, applicable and an intricate part of Christian faith today.

In reflecting on these virtues, I believe you will find a way to unite that which is so often divided and portrayed as being in conflict and opposition in our daily lives—the heart and the mind. Lewis shows us in his book that these need not be in opposition, and in bringing them together, we may find the Kingdom of God is at hand and all around us. I hope and pray that you will find that balance in your lives.

Contents

Introduction iv
No Man is an Island 1
   Reflections on Lewis's Voyage 1
   Personal Ponderings 5
   Finding Scripture 7
Don't Fight. Push. 10
   Reflections on Lewis's Voyage 10
   Personal Ponderings 13
Look Before You Leap 18
   Reflections on Lewis's Voyage 18
   Personal Ponderings 21
Guard Your Dreams 24
   Reflections on Lewis's Voyage 24
   Personal Ponderings 27
Hearing God's Will 32
   Reflections on Lewis's Voyage 32
   Personal Ponderings 34
Food for the Journey 39
   Reflections on Lewis's Voyage 39
   Personal Ponderings 40
Entering God's Kingdom 45
   Reflections on Lewis's Voyage 45
   Personal Ponderings 47
Negating the Negative 50
   Reflections on Lewis's Voyage 50
   Personal Ponderings 52

Troubled with Treasure 56
    Reflections on Lewis's Voyage 56
    Personal Ponderings 57
Facing God 60
    Reflections on Lewis's Voyage 60
    Personal Ponderings 61
Conquering Curiosity 64
    Reflections on Lewis's Voyage 64
    Personal Ponderings 65
Loving Ourselves as We Are 69
    Reflections on Lewis's Voyage 69
    Personal Ponderings 70
Seeing Others' Suffering 74
    Reflections on Lewis's Voyage 74
    Personal Ponderings 76
Going it Alone 80
    Reflections on Lewis's Voyage 80
    Personal Ponderings 83
The Voice of Intervention 87
    Reflections on Lewis's Voyage 87
    Personal Ponderings 88
Letting Go of Ourselves 92
    Reflections on Lewis's Voyage 92
    Personal Ponderings 93
Facing Darkness 96
    Reflections on Lewis's Voyage 96
    Personal Ponderings 100

Finding Prayer 103
    Reflections on Lewis's Voyage 103
    Personal Ponderings 106

Friends and Enemies 111
    Reflections on Lewis's Voyage 111
    Personal Ponderings 112

Worried Sick 115
    Reflections on Lewis's Voyage 115
    Personal Ponderings 117

Making Laws Just 121
    Reflections on Lewis's Voyage 121
    Personal Ponderings 122

Delivering Grace to the Ungracious 125
    Reflections on Lewis's Voyage 125
    Personal Ponderings 126

Learning to Listen 130
    Reflections on Lewis's Voyage 130
    Personal Ponderings 131

Called to Serve 134
    Reflections on Lewis's Voyage 134
    Personal Ponderings 135

Wise Counsel 138
    Reflections on Lewis's Voyage 138
    Personal Ponderings 139

Leaving No One Behind 142
    Reflections on Lewis's Voyage 142
    Personal Ponderings 143

Delivering from Danger 146
    Reflections on Lewis's Voyage 146
Closing Thoughts 150
Endnotes 151
    Section One 151
    Section Two 155
    Section Three 157
    Section Four 160
Bibliography 163

SECTION ONE: PONDERING PRUDENCE

Prudence means practical commonsense, taking the trouble to think out what you are doing and what is likely to come of it.[1]

NO MAN IS AN ISLAND

REFLECTIONS ON LEWIS'S VOYAGE

In Eustace's diary, we find him to be negative, depressed, and melancholy. He tends to be one who finds fault in everyone and everything. He complains that his shipmates can't "count right," and that he doesn't get "proper meals," feels "rotten all day," and has to deal with the "interfering prig Edmund," "odious stuck-up prig" Caspian, and the "little spy, Reep." He describes the voyage as "dangerous" and claims to be having "a ghastly time, up and down enormous waves hour after hour, usually wet to the skin."[2] While we might be disappointed in and annoyed by Eustace, don't you also see some of your own times of ranting? I am sure that Lewis must have seen part of himself in Eustace. For in *Surprised by Joy*, he tells us that when he considered himself an atheist his "view was closely connected with a certain lopsidedness of temperament." He confesses: "I had always been more violent in my negative than in my positive demands."[3] Thus, the character of Eustace seems to present us with a lesson. In story form, Lewis shows us where there the pessimist might end up. And ironically (because Lewis could not have foreseen future events), Eustace's diary ends with September 11. Looking back on the story now, that date stirs a powerful reminder of just where negative and hateful feelings can lead.

And where does Eustace eventually find himself? Lost, alone, disconnected, and in the form of a dragon. His negativity leads him to a selfishness that entices him to wander off alone in an attempt to get out of work. Yet, when he seeks to return to the others—he can't. He has created too much distance. Lewis symbolically depicts this by turning him into a dragon—from which his shipmates initially fear and seek to flee. Additionally, his selfishness and greed is displayed in the bracelet that cannot be removed from his arm. In greedily hoarding jewelry and treasure for himself, he slid the bracelet onto his arm. But as a dragon, the bracelet is a useless, tight, and painful reminder of the selfish beast he has become.

Lewis scripts Eustace's rapid descent from negativity into lonely isolation with metaphorical images that create a lasting impression. After wandering off alone, "the fog from the mountains closed in all round him." He then "for the first time in his life" begins "to feel lonely." And his loneliness "grew very gradually" to "worry," which causes him to leap "into panic" and "beg[i]n the descent," which Lewis chooses to describe as "slithering down a slide of loose stones" leading to an "unknown valley" where "the sea was no where in sight."[4]

As Christians, we easily associate the words of panic, worry, lonely, and descent with the images of fog, slithering, loose stones, unknown valley, and no sea with sin. Eustace's "slithering" reminds us of Satan. The "loose stones" show a lack of faith. An "unknown valley" where "the sea was no where in sight" could only be seen as hell. In Eustace's descent, Lewis reflects on his own descent to atheism and calls us to reflect on how we are viewing our own life circumstances. Are we also inclined to look at the negative? Do we tend to isolate ourselves from others? If this is the case, Lewis shows us where we may "descend" if we don't change the way we look at life and interact with others. We may also find ourselves lonely, lost, and in an unknown valley.

A Change of View

How do we change the way we look at life? How do we avoid the negative? Lewis offers advice to his friend Arthur Greeves on this in his letters. While serving in the trenches and on the front line during war, Lewis learned to see life differently. In fact he admits to Greeves "my views have changed."[5] By a change of view he is referring to his equation "Matter = Nature = Satan." On the opposite side of the equation, he places "beauty," which he notes as "the only spiritual & non-natural" he has "yet found."[6]

While this may seem a bit confusing at first and opposite what he says about nature in *Surprised by Joy*, his explanations of the equation to Greeves help to clarify and give us insight into how we may also change our view. Greeves, voicing our own questions, argues in response to Lewis that nature is beautiful—and thus also part of the equation and impossible to be linked with evil. To this Lewis responds by using the example of a tree. He says that we only call it beautiful because of its "shape, colour, and motions, and perhaps a little because of association." These "sensations" are "produced vibrations on the aether between me and the tree: the real tree is something quite different—a combination of colourless, shapeless, invisible atoms."[7] Thus, Lewis concludes that:

> ... neither the tree, nor any other object can be beautiful in itself.... The beauty therefore is not in the matter at all, but is something purely spiritual, arising mysteriously out of the relation between me & the tree: or perhaps ... out of some indwelling spirit behind the tree.... And Beauty is the call of the spirit in that something to the spirit to us.[8]

And here we get the first glimpse of Lewis's admission that there is some sort of spirit at work in this world. Of this he says:

> I do believe that I have in me a spirit, a chip shall we say, of universal spirit; and that, since all good & joyful things are spiritual & non-material, I must be careful not to let matter (=nature=Satan, remember) get too great a hold on me, & dull the one spark I have.[9]

If you find this confusing and philosophical, you are not alone. Greeves and Lewis continued the discussion for several letters. In these letters, Lewis explains that our bodies are limited by our senses. In other words, we know the world by how our brain translates it—this limits us to know it only in one way. We know leaves to be green because that is how our eyes see the color, but without our eyes the leaves are colorless. We only know what our body and brain can translate, and we are limited to these translations. There may be more to the tree that our senses cannot know. He finds danger in focusing only on these limited translations. Focusing on matter and our body's translation of matter is not what gives us joy—it is our relationship with it. The stirring it raises in us. This is where beauty is found and where we meet the spiritual. Later, he finds this Spirit to be God.

So why does he bring Satan into this equation? To answer this, we return to Eustace. He only looks at the matter of nature—what his brain translates (usually negatively and with a limited perspective). And in the translations, he finds displeasure. Thus, Satan is able to mislead him into descent. But, if we look beyond the matter and at our relationship with the matter, we will become in touch with the spiritual sensations of our world and with the feelings of joy. Thus, to avoid this pitfall, we must change our view.

Another bit of advice that Lewis gives Greeves (November 1917) comes from Robert Burton's book, *The Anatomy of Melancholy* (1621). He reminds him that Burton advises " 'be not idle, be not solitary.'"[10] Lewis touches on this again almost a year later in another letter when he says "interesting and arduous work is about the one thing to save us from melancholy."[11] Again, applying this to Eustace, you remember that he wandered off alone to avoid work and thus went from melancholy to panic. Here, we find that work is good and healthy. Additionally, we see that we were not intended to be alone.

We should not isolate ourselves from our family, friends, and community.

Personal Ponderings

In Another World

Lewis's example of Eustace and perceptions about isolation and nature take on human form when we consider the story of Helen Keller. While she had a short year of hearing and seeing, the remainder of her life was lived with an inability to hear and see after an acute congestion of the stomach and brain left her both deaf and blind. In her autobiography, *The Story of My Life,* Keller remembers the loss of her hearing and seeing as "like a nightmare," the worst part of it feeling as though she had been surrounded in silence and darkness.[12]

As she continued to age with the crude use of signs, she became very "vexed" as she realized that her family members could communicate, while she could not. She describes herself as standing "between two persons who were conversing" and as she "touched their lips," she could not understand. When she tried to imitate them by moving her own lips "frantically without result," she says that she angrily kicked and screamed herself into exhaustion.[13] Interestingly, she describes these days as like being "at sea in a dense fog, when it seemed as if a tangible white darkness shut you in." In her isolation, she recalls that "anger and bitterness had preyed upon [her] continually."[14] Does this not remind you of Eustace's bad temperament and of the fog that surrounded him after he wandered off alone? And don't her frantic efforts to communicate remind you of Eustace's panic at finding himself lost from the others? In their isolation, we are reminded of our need to be able to communicate with others. While Keller's was not self-inflicted as Eustace's was, their isolation from others leads to an emotional descent. Keller tells us that "in the still, dark world in which [she] lived there was no strong sentiment or tenderness."[15]

It wasn't until Annie Sullivan was able to help Keller connect the "w-a-t-e-r" spelled into her hand to the flowing, cool stream in her other hand that Keller was able to feel "a misty consciousness as of something forgotten—a thrill of returning thought." Keller describes this moment as "an awakening of her soul." From that moment on everything she touched "quivered with life." [16] Here, Keller seems to find naturally what we struggled to take away from Lewis's explanation of matter and nature. In identifying water, she doesn't find an awakening because of the matter of water. Her awakening brought her (like Lewis) what she describes as "joy." And she tells us that the more things she "handled" and "learned" the "more joyous and confident grew [her] sense of kinship with the rest of the world."[17] I think it is interesting to note here that she focuses on her "kinship with the rest of the world" because it is very similar to Lewis's description of feeling a relationship to the spirit of nature. Both examples show us that we must look beyond nature and matter to find happiness. We do not find joy in the object itself but in what relationship it forms with us. Keller exemplifies what Lewis was trying to convey to Greeves—we do not need to rely on our eyesight or the matter of the object to find these stirrings of joy.

Also, like Lewis, Keller finds "beauty" and a spirit in nature. She says that Sullivan taught her to "find beauty in the fragrant woods, in every blade of the grass, and in the curves of dimples of [her] baby sister's hand." She recalls that Sullivan made her to feel as though nature was "a happy peer."[18] As an example of this, she describes a spring morning where she "instinctively stretched out [her] hands. It seemed as if the spirit of spring had passed through the summerhouse."[19]

Later, Keller was able to pull from her these stirrings and feelings to understand the abstract concept of love. In the way that she could not see or touch the feelings that nature arose in her, she would find that she couldn't touch love. She remembered Sullivan explaining "you cannot touch love ... but you feel the sweetness that it pours into everything. Without love you would not be happy or want to play." And in making the connection between her feelings from nature and the feeling of love, "a beautiful truth burst upon [her] mind ... invisible lines stretched between [her] spirit and the spirit of others."[20] Perhaps, in her blindness and deafness, Keller has an advantage over us. She seems to naturally find what lies beyond the physical matter of nature. In exploring her world, she naturally finds a connection to the spirit of nature and the spirits of other. This connection brings her joyfully out of her dark and lonely fog of isolation.

Finding Purpose

When do you tend to become negative in your thinking?

How has this isolated you from others? From God?

How did you find your way out of your darkness?

What type of work are you most likely to avoid? Why?

Describe a time when you found work to drive away your melancholy?

When have you felt a spiritual presence in nature? How did it deepen your relationship with God? With others?

FINDING SCRIPTURE

While there is much to be learned from the lessons of Eustace, Lewis, and Helen Keller about our need to be surrounded with and able to communicate with others, Genesis offers us the origin of this lesson. For in reading the second creation story, we hear from God that it is not good for us to be alone (Genesis 3:18). And thus he begetted woman from man's own rib—making them out of the same flesh and bone (Genesis 3:23). And they are happy, until ... like Eustace, Eve begins to reflect on what she doesn't have. The serpent cunningly convinces her to focus on the matter of the tree of knowledge of good and evil as something which she doesn't not have and thus must be good in itself. As Lewis noted in his equation matter=nature=Satan, Eve allows Satan to direct her sight on only the material make up of the tree. The serpent then reminds her that this is something she cannot have and causes her thinking and view to be negative and melancholy. He then cleverly channels these feelings into an anger toward God—leading her to eat from the tree in disobedience. She then continues the cycle and models the behavior of Satan by enticing Adam to also eat of the tree. The result is isolation from God and from the garden. And in this isolation they also find pain, strife, and death.

Do you not see the same message here that Lewis found to be true with himself and depicts in the character of Eustace? By directing our sight on only the material composition of objects, Satan is able to direct our thoughts and values to what he have and do not have. Our attitude becomes negative and melancholy because the material object becomes the object of our desire, and thus we miss all the stirrings of joy and contentment that could come from feeling the relationship we have with it. And like Lewis and Eustace, Eve's unhappiness with what she had and desire for more lead her and Adam into sin. They isolated themselves from God and the garden which was intended to bring them great joy.

So how are we to avoid this? It will not be easy, especially when the media constantly bombards us with the material as the means of happiness. We will need to work to change our view of life and look beyond the material and focus on the spiritual. We will need to ignore the messages of media that emphasis the self rather than the community. We will need to turn to God and to the spirit at work in each other and nature to find the peace and happiness that God intended us to find.

Suggested Scripture Reading & Reflections
Read Genesis 2 and 3 to further reflect on how the serpent was able to lead Adam and Eve into sin and isolation. The following questions may serve as an useful guide for your reflections:

What material items are you most likely to focus on?

How is Satan able to trick you into believing they will bring you happiness?

What types of feelings and thoughts do you usually experience when you focus on the material?

Describe a time that you were able to look beyond the material of nature. What feelings did you experience?

What most isolates you from others? From God?

When have you found "Beauty"? How did it improve your relationships with others?

10

Don't Fight. Push.

Reflections on Lewis's Voyage

When the ugly and monstrous Sea Serpent raises its head above the *Dawn Treader,* the entire crew finds itself fearful and in turmoil. Their first instinct is vocalized by the Master Bowman, as he screams " 'Shoot! Shoot!'"[21] As the ship soon finds itself "under the arch of the serpent," others clamor into action. Even Eustace finds the courage to help his crew as he thrusts one of Caspian's sword into the beast. But the sword breaks and they appear to be losing the battle. It isn't until Reepicheep wisely stops and ponders the situation and their actions. Contrary to his fighting and zealous nature, he calls out "'Don't fight! Push!'"[22] The others are so astounded by this unusual and unnatural advice coming from Reepicheep that they stop for a brief moment and pause. As they watch him push on the loop of the serpent's tail, they understand his advice. The loop of the tail was tightly closing in on the stern of the ship and would soon cause the stern to snap. Fighting the beast would only allow it to tighten its grip. In Reepicheep's assessment of the situation, he found the prudence to stop the fighting and begin pushing.

Comparing the religious parallels of this situation to our own and Lewis's, we might also discover how to apply prudence to our own spiritual battles. First, look at the sea serpent. Clearly, the monster could only represent Satan—the serpent from Genesis. The raising of his ugly head in the waters of the sea mirrors the occasions when he suddenly appears in our lives attempting to wreak havoc. The fact that his head is described as shooting out "level with the mast"[23] symbolically reflects his attack on our faith—often represented with a cross (the same shape as a mast). The Master Bowman—again the bow resembling a cross—causes us to reflect on ourselves as Christians and our instinctive attempts to shoot back at Satan with crossfire. Eustace's noble and selfless attempts to slay the dragon reflect the same. But here, Reepicheep ... the one most apt to fight ... takes pause to reflect and assess the situation. Prudently, he finds that fighting back will only allow the serpent to win. In fact, he likely expects and wants the crew to fight.

So what is the lesson? Our initial instinct to retaliate may lead to our destruction. Instead, like Reepicheep, we need to restrain this urge and wisely (and sometimes quickly) prudently think out the best line of defense. Sometimes this might require us to "push!" And in "push," I find Lewis telling us *to push ourselves and others* to find the best possible solution. This often requires us to *push against* our desire to fight. Because as illustrated in this scene, those instincts to fight might in fact bring about our own destruction and the destruction of others.

We might best see evidence of Lewis learning this lesson in his relationship with his own father. Unfortunately, Lewis didn't take the time to prudently and wisely push against his natural instincts. While they didn't physically and verbally abuse one another, they did create an unnecessary emotional distance to retaliate with one another on hurts of the past. Warren tells us of this emotional estrangement in his memoir of his brother in *Letters of C.S. Lewis*. He explains that C.S. Lewis was deeply hurt that his father did not make an effort to see him before he went off to war—for what Warren notes "may very well have been a last meeting." Warren also notes the hurt and pain his brother felt when his father did not come to visit him in the hospital after he was wounded in war. [24]

Walter Hooper also calls attention to this estrangement in his footnotes in *They Stand Together*. Hooper adds even more dimension to the discord by including information from Albert Lewis's diary. In various entries, Albert discusses his displeasure with his son's relationship with Mrs. Moore.[25] Interestingly, Warren blames his brother's relationship with Mrs. Moore on their father. He believes that Lewis clung to her as a mother figure for the affection he never received from his father—especially after his father failed to see him off for war or visit him in the hospital.[26]

Hooper also writes of an instance where Albert and C.S. argued over money. Albert discovered that his son had lied to him about his finances and was actually overdrawn in his account. According to Albert, when he questioned his son about the lie, C. S. defensively blamed his father for never giving him his confidence and for all of the mistreatment his father gave him in his childhood. According to Hooper, it was years before they ever really got beyond this fight.[27] And in Lewis's letters to Greeves, it is easy to see the effects of the estrangement. He sarcastically refers to his father as "Excellenz" and often has Greeves serve as the go-between with his father—to avoid communicating with him whenever possible. [28]

It isn't until years later, when his father is dying that Lewis is able to let go of retaliatory instincts that are fueled by hurt and pride. Then he prudently ponders the situation and realizes that he and his father "are physical counterparts." In reflecting on this realization to his friend Owen Barfield, he says "... during these days more than ever I notice his resemblance to me."[29] Unfortunately, his father soon passed away after this reflection. And then when he is finally free from his father's scrutiny and free to do whatever he likes, Lewis finds it "beastly."

The irony of this is that in dealing with difficult people other than his father he is able to look beyond their faults. In a letter written during the height of his discord with his father, he tells Greeves that he has discovered when finding "an objectionable feature" present in an "author or people we meet" we can best overlook this if we "trace it back to some central point of character from which it originates."[31] Perhaps tracing the objectionable trait of his father to its origin would have caused him to also look at the same trait in himself—and this may have been too difficult. This takes us back to the notion of "push." We must push ourselves to look even when it means looking at ourselves. Lewis eventually found the courage to let go of his retaliating and to prudently push himself to ponder the source of the feuding—but not until his father was dying. While this is better than never, it would have been better if he could have pushed himself sooner. And perhaps there we find our own lesson.

Personal Ponderings

Passive Resistance

I can't think of a better nonfiction personification of Reepicheep's command "Don't Fight! Push!" than Mohandas Karamchand Gandhi. Born in 1869 to a Bania family in Porbunder, Kathiawar, Gandhi eventually became a lawyer and was engaged by a Muslim firm in 1893 to travel on legal business to South Africa. While most likely finding himself surrounded by an alien culture while living there, he found himself greatly moved by the strife and injustice inflicted upon many of the Indians in South Africa. Determined to bring about freedom for all, he decided to stay to protest race and discrimination. Fueling his protest were works of religious literature, including the Bible, the Koran and Tolstoy's *The Kingdom of God is Within You*.[32]

As part of this movement he founded the Natal Indian Congress. To gather further support for his cause, he returned to India in July of 1896 and then later returned to South Africa with his wife and children in November of 1896. The hallmarks of his protests were his calls for passive resistance and nonviolence. His resistance often involved resisting laws of registration, marching and writing in protest of racist laws and practices. Later in 1915, he returned to India where he also lived out his philosophies of passive resistance to the unjust laws.[33]

Visiting Gandhi in what he describes as a "sizzling Indian village" in the summer of 1942, biographer Louis Fisher was impressed with Gandhi's work to "wean the caste Hindu from his cruel mistreatment of the Untouchables." Fisher was also aghast at the hundreds of visitors who sought Gandhi's advice and wisdom. He recalls that to all of them Gandhi listened and offered his wise words of peace. Reading Fisher's reflections and observations of some of the meetings, I am amazed at the diversity of Gandhi's guests—ranging from married couples seeking marital advice, peasants and workingmen, to educators and Congress Prime Ministers of Indian provinces. All were welcomed, respected, and listened to.[34]

In Gandhi's philosophy of non-violence, we also see the words and teachings of Christ. As a follower of *ahimsa,* which Gandhi defines as "the largest love, greatest charity," he applies "the same rules to the wrong-doer" as to "[his] wrong-doing father or son." To live like this, he calls upon "truth and fearlessness," for one "cannot practice[sic] ahimsa and be a coward at the same time. The practice of ahimsa calls forth the greatest courage."[35]

Applying Gandhi's words to the situation of Reepicheep, we see the valiant mouse learning that courage might best be shown by putting down our arms and rallying others to resist the force of evil in more wise ways. Prudence allows him to realize that they must "push" or in Gandhi's terms "resist," in order to break the monster's release on the ship. Fighting would have only resulted in the destruction of the ship and the entire crew.

Applying the words of Gandhi to the situation of Lewis and his father, Gandhi's advice for us to love our enemies and strangers as we would our fathers and sons becomes somewhat paradoxical because Lewis and his father were often more patient and kind toward their enemies and strangers than they were with each other. But don't you also find this to be true? I know I do. Unfortunately, I often treat strangers with greater patience and kindness than I do my own family members. Reflecting on these words, I shamefully realize that I have much growing to do in loving my family. I must put down my intolerant arms and "push" myself to reach out with open arms of love.

Finding Purpose

In his autobiography, Gandhi recalls the example of his mother's "saintliness" as having a lasting impression on him. Who has modeled love, faith, and self-sacrifice for you?

What examples are you modeling for others?

Gandhi and Lewis both note being influenced by their reading? What do you read? How has it shaped your life?

How might you apply Reepicheep's command of "Don't fight! Push!" to your own life?

When will this be most challenging?

How will you meet this challenge?

Finding Scripture

Love Your Enemies

There is good reason for Gandhi's embrace of passive resistance to remind us of our Christian teachings, for they share the same commandment to love. Christ tells us in his Sermon on the Mount that we are to love those who mistreat us. Interestingly, in his autobiography *The Story of My Experiments with Truth,* Gandhi explains that Christ's teachings in this sermon had an immediate and profound impact on him. He says that he found great appeal in the fact that "renunciation was the highest form of religion."[36] One can also see how these teachings later combined with his embracement of ahimsa—as discussed above—and his eventual protests of passive resistance to bring justice to the oppressed.

For Christians, the Sermon of the Mount challenges us daily. It calls us to love everyone—even those who are unkind and cruel to us. We are also called to live our lives serving others and God. Certainly this takes a different kind of courage than that of "fighting." This challenge requires us to "push" ourselves to act with patience, kindness, forgiveness and self-sacrifice. Christ modeled this on the highest level when he endured persecution and while enduring it prayed for and forgave the very ones persecuting him. He sacrificed his life for us so that we may live. In turn, he asks the same of us. Gandhi learned to live these challenges throughout the course of his life. He took his teachings from religious writings and the Bible. We are called to do the same.

Suggested Scripture Reading and Reflections

To continue with this challenge, read and ponder Luke 6:20-36. Then, read Luke 23:33-47. As you read the passages, reflect on how God is calling you to "push" yourself and others to act out his commandments of love and nonviolence.

When are you most likely to lash out at others in anger? Why?

What is usually the result of lashing out in anger and defense?

What makes it so difficult to act with love and selflessness?

Why is it sometimes harder to treat our loved ones with kindness?

How can you "push" yourself to take the time to pause and think out more peaceful solutions to your conflicts?

Jesus loved his persecutors and forgave them even in his moments of greatest pain and suffering. How can you find the courage to love as Jesus loved?

Look Before You Leap

Reflections on Lewis's Voyage

For most of us, jumping to conclusions is our constant exercise. Advertisers train us in this every day. Buy this shampoo and your hair will be the silkiest and softest—making you the envy of everyone in the office. Drive this car and you will have complete freedom. Wear these jeans and all of the women will be looking at you with desire. How often do we really pick apart the logic of these advertisements that constantly bombard us? Seldom. In fact, we don't even question. Our subconscious stores the message, and we buy the message and the product. Without realizing it, we seek out the product in the store and purchase, believing that it will provide us with some sort of happiness.

But prudence tells us to stop and question these messages. When we do, we realize the multiple flaws of their logic. Does our hair, jeans, and car really determine who we are? Do we really want relationships with people who seek us out because of these items? And our faith reminds us that nothing material can bring us happiness—nor should we be seeking the type of happiness that the advertisements are selling. Doesn't an overconcern with our hair, clothes, and car reek of vanity and pride? Aren't those thought to be deadly sins? Business advertising, with its quick images of promises of instant happiness, tricks us into forgetting all of those questions. But, if we are to remain strong and constant in our faith, we need to have the prudence to question those images.

In reflecting on the trends of our modern culture in an interview on May 5, 1963 with Sherwood Eliot Wirt, Lewis remarked that recent appearances of filth and obscenity in literature "were a sign of a culture that has lost its faith. Moral collapse follows upon spiritual collapse." In looking to future trends, he had "great apprehension."

In support of his views, he remarked to Wirt that "The Gospel is something completely different. In fact, it is directly opposed to the world." [37]

Yet, I believe Lewis began offering advice in regards to this much sooner than this 1963 interview. In *The Voyage of the Dawn Treader,* we receive many examples and reminders of how we should be more prudent. One scene that reminds us to stop and think before reaching for the gold, comes when the crew of the *Dawn Treader* comes across a deep, clear pool of water in the middle of cliffs. The crew is hot, thirsty and tired. Lewis tells us that no doubt they must have been tempted to jump into the pool for a quick and refreshing bath. Eustace was even on the verge of dipping his hand into water for a drink. But he is interrupted by what they saw when they looked down into the water. Do you remember what they saw at the bottom of the pool? A gold statue of a man with his back on the floor of the pool—his hands outstretched. It was lit up so beautifully from the sun that Lucy proclaims it to be "the most beautiful she had ever seen."[38] Caspian agrees and eagerly wants to retrieve it as he asks "can we get it out?"[39]

Here don't you somewhat see ourselves? The crew is tired and thirsty from their journey, as we are often tired and thirsty on our own spiritual journey. And sometimes, this leads us to be tempted to drink from the water of this world to quench our thirst—like Eustace. Or we may be tempted by the glittering gold treasures that reside in the waters of this world. When we see the beautiful images and ads flit across the screens of our televisions and computers, inside magazines, and on bulletin boards, we want to dive in to retrieve those items. But ... prudence tells us to stop and think before we leap.

And ironically, Edmund (who had been tempted and tricked by the white witch in the first book), displays this type of prudence.

When the valiant and brave Reepicheep says "We dive for it, Sire," Edmund responds "No good at all." He then tells them to first "see what the depth *is* like."[40] While on a literal level, he is referring to the depth of the pool. Symbolically and metaphorically, we can apply this to the depth of our desires and the material waters of our world. If we check the depth, we will find the water to be somewhat face value and superficial.

Edmund's prudent decision to stop and check the depth out first proves very valuable. For they discover that the water turns everything that touches it into gold. Thus, the Narnian lord who gave into the temptations of the water and failed to prudently think out his decision before he leapt into the pool found himself turned to gold—and there he met his death. I wonder if we aren't heading toward a similar demise—in drinking from the golden waters of this world rather than the spiritual waters of our baptisms are we also meeting our spiritual deaths?

In fact, while writing this, I stopped to answer the ringing telephone. I had to smile as on the other line a jeweler spurted off their latest jewelry specials. I thought of the scene I just described of the gold statue and Edmund's prudence to test the depth of the waters, as she with genuine concern told me of her desire to meet all of my "jewelry needs." Today, I was able to laugh at the notion of "jewelry" being a need. Yet, on another day, might I fall for prey to the advertisement and buy into their promotion. Tempted that I really need a new gold chain to hold my cross pendant, or that I really need a new watch to wear to work, might I convince myself the phone call was a blessing? Honestly, I know that I might.

Personal Ponderings
The Wrong Kind of Happiness?

    I can't help but wonder if our recent increase in childhood obesity does not show evidence of constant search for happiness in this world. While researchers blame junk food and lack of exercise, shouldn't we look deeper—to discover the reason for an increased consumption of junk food and a lack of physical exercise? Certainly, junk food and lack of exercise causes weight gain. But, why are our children eating so much and exercising so little? Could they be buying into the lies that advertising and our material world sends them? Do they believe that food and video games will bring them happiness? Are they looking for that quick, superficial fix for happiness? Is that the message that we are sending when we place vending machines in our schools and purchase expensive entertainment and video game systems for our children? Are we teaching them that these types of activities and foods will give them lasting happiness?

    Statistics show that since 1980, the percentage of children defined as obese has climbed from 6.5 percent to 17 percent.[41] While there is some optimism that for the first time since 1980 there seems to be a plateau in this increase,[42] shouldn't these figures give us cause to pause and ponder? Where are we seeking happiness? Where are we telling our children to find happiness? Jesus told us that we cannot live by bread alone. Clearly, this is not the message we are sending our children. Perhaps, Lewis had good reason to look to the not too distant future of today with apprehension and horror.

Finding Purpose

    While Caspian and Reepicheep are eager to jump into the pool to retrieve the beautiful gold statue, Edmund wisely stops to pause and ponder before leaping into the pool water. Had they jumped in, they would have been turned to gold and perished at the bottom of the pool. When have you been like Caspian and Reepicheep? What was the result?

When have you stopped and pondered before making a decision and leaping in haphazardly? What did you discover in your ponderings?

Why are we so quick to leap before thinking?

What material items tempt you from the waters of this world? Why do they tempt you? What does this reveal about your wants and desires?

When you check the depth of the water, what do you discover?

What do you most need to pull from your baptismal waters to quench the thirst of your spiritual journey?

Finding Scripture

The Golden Calf

In Exodus 32, we discover that not much has really changed. When the people God led out of Egypt grow anxious and weary waiting for Moses to return from the mountain, they beg Aaron to quickly give them another God to worship. Do you not see our own desire for instant gratification here, as well as our tendency to worship and place trust in the false golden idols of this material world?

The preceding chapter (Exodus 31) shows us that God does not find gold or material items intrinsically bad. In fact, he acknowledges to have given Bezalel from the tribe of Juday and Oholiab from the tribe of Dan the skills of artisans to make a tent and ark of the covenant and furnish them. But in reading the two chapters together, we see that gold and material items are not to be worshipped in themselves. Rather, they are intended to honor and give glory to God.

God becomes angry with the worshiping of the Golden Calf and his people's impatience and inability to remain true to God—who had delivered them out of the Egypt. Moses pleads with God to spare them his wrath. If God was angered with their false idol worship and lack of faith in him, will He not also be angered with our own seeking after material items? Does He not try to teach us here to rely on him for our happiness?

Suggested Scripture Reading and Reflections

To further ponder how we are led astray after our own golden statues, read Exodus 31 and 32. Then reflect on the following questions:

What golden statues do you worship? Why?

When have you become impatient with God? Why?

How did you deal with this impatience?

When have others turned to you in their impatience with God? How did you respond?

When have you been like Aaron and caved in to others' impatience? What was the result?

What can you do to be more prudent in avoiding the temptation to turn to false gods for happiness and security?

Guard Your Dreams

Reflections on Lewis's Voyage

Surely, all of us day dream. We think of how magnificent our lives could be—if only we had _____, and _____, and don't forget _____. Soon, we discover that our list of desires has no end. And soon, we find ourselves depressed, forlorn, and desolate. We feel as though we are neglected and will never have the happiness we truly desire. We then begin a pity party for ourselves where we dwell on all of the horrible and rotten moments of our lives. We lose all hope and become swallowed by the darkness. Fortunately, most of us find our way out. Someone comes along to pull us up out of the dark and dreadful waters. They help us to see the goodness and grace of God—we then feel ashamed for not realizing all that we have been blessed with.

For many years, Lewis found himself swallowed in this type of darkness—a darkness that sucked out his faith in God. In his letters to friends and in his autobiography *Surprised by Joy*, we find that he lived in this darkness as an atheist for many years—dwelling on the loss of his mother, the alienation he felt from his grieving father, and the abuses that he suffered in the school system. To find some light, he sought to be a famous author. But, this success never really came until his friends helped him find his way back to God. Once he found the light of Christianity, his writing centered on God's message of love and eternal life. He found hope and led others out of darkness with his writings. For example, his Christian radio talks during World War II offered much light to a dark and wounded world. Finally, he found success. But the irony is, he was no longer seeking it. He was seeking to do God's will. He sought God's mercy not material wealth and success.

In *Voyage of the Dawn Treader,* Lewis gives us a glimpse of what his journey from darkness must have been like. When the crew of the *Dawn Treader* journeys into the dark waters of the Island of Darkness at the brave urgings of Reepicheep, we are told that to picture the darkness by imagining ourselves "looking into the mouth of a railway tunnel."[43] Reading this description, I couldn't help but recall Lewis's description of Campbell College where he endured bullying and became ill as "like living in a large railway station."[44] In pairing these two descriptions with Lewis's belief that "We cannot speak, perhaps we can hardly think, of an 'inner conflict' without a metaphor …. And as the conflict becomes more and more important, it is inevitable that these metaphors should expand and coalesce."[45] Here, we see Lewis at Campbell College begin to enter the tunnel that would eventually lead to the Dark Island he found at Wyvern.

He tells us in *Surprised by Joy* that his journey to darkness had already begun with his mother's death and the "seeds" of "deeply ingrained pessimism" that began with his inability to "cut a straight line" and "bred" in him "a deep sense of resistance or opposition of inanimate things."[46] At a young age, he grew frustrated that things in our world were beyond his control. Prayer did not stop his mother's death, and with his "clumsy hands" he could not produce the "straight line" he desired. Thus, he began the gradual decline to despair that I mentioned earlier—and that we all are vulnerable to also. In his despair and lack of control, he found the "universe evil."[47]

Adding to these frustrations, Lewis names a few other factors leading to his journey to darkness. In looking toward his future as an adult, he could only see what his father foresaw as the inevitable future for all adults—"an unremitting struggle in which the best [he] could hope for was to avoid the workinghouse."[48] He said that these thoughts "sunk deeply" into his "mind," because he never had the prudence to see that other adults were thriving and avoiding such awful outcomes.[49] This pessimistic disposition was further fueled by authors such as Sir Robert Ball and H.G. Wells whose works "lodged firmly" in his "imagination" the "vastness and coldness of space, the littleness of Man."[50] Such stirrings of his imagination, led his already "Atheistical thought" to seek happiness and pleasure in "Occultist fancies."[51] There, he dropped his faith with a sense of relief—much like the man the *Dawn Treader* encountered in the dark waters who tells them that he had been drawn to the island because of its ability to make all "Dreams come true."[52] Lewis, frustrated with a faith that did not allow him the ability to control his world like a god, sought out fantasies in the occult and mythology that allowed him to feel godlike.

And then at Wyvern, also much like the man who sought the happiness at the Island where dreams come true, Lewis found himself seeking "glitter, swagger, distinction, the desire to be in the know."[53] However, also like the man from the island, Lewis hadn't prudently considered that would also include nightmares. And Lewis, finally completing his journey at Wyvern found himself in dark waters of "oppression"[54] where he was "almost wholly dominated by the social struggle."[55] And there he learned the lesson that eventually led him to later turn to God—much like the crew heard the man in the water cry out "Mercy! Even if you are only one more dream have mercy. Take me on board."[56] What was the lesson? Lewis states it best: "The World will only lead you to Hell."[57] Here on earth, we may also find our dreams leading us on a journey that leads us to darkness and personal torment. Lewis uses this scene of the man in dark waters to show us his own dark journey, which his biographer Roger Green agrees, Lewis "turned to very good and convincing use in the chapter called "The Dark Island" in *The Voyage of the Dawn Treader*.[58]

So how do we avoid such a nightmarish journey? Lewis gives some advice to his friend Greeves when he describes the mental anguish and "neurasthenia" that Mrs. Moore's brother, Dr. John Askins, experienced while staying with Lewis and Mrs. Moore. For the three weeks he was there, he "endured awful mental tortures" that could have easily been mistaken for "lunacy" and "horrible manic fits" where he thought "he was going to Hell." Concerned by what he witnessed, he tells Greeves that both he and Greeves may be prone to it because they were both "afraid of their fathers as children." He says to avoid it they must keep to "work," "open air," and to look on the "cheerful & matter of fact side of things." And "above all beware of excessive day dreaming, of seeing yourself in the centre of drama, of self pity, and, as far as possible, of fears." [59]

Personal Ponderings

When Nightmares Come True

Lewis's advice takes on a new meaning for me today as I read the many testimonies from those in Iowa communities who found their homes obliterated from last weekend's round of Memorial Day tornadoes. The National Weather Service described the tornado that destroyed half of Parkersburg Iowa as "the state's strongest twister in 32 years." It claimed seven lives and left hundreds of people homeless as it tore through Parkersburg and nearby towns with winds of 205 mph. Rated as an F5 tornado (the highest rating), it is the strongest tornado the United States has seen since the Kansas tornado on May 4, 2007 claimed 11 lives. [60]

Their stories and struggles send chills up my spine, as I realize how close this tornado came to my own home. I live about half an hour's drive from all of the communities that were hit. So I am constantly struck with the thought—"that could have been me." Yet, quickly, I take Lewis's advice and refuse to place myself in center of the drama, or to give in to fears—as we head into tornado season. Rather, I turn my eyes to the faith of these people as they rummage through the little that is left of their belongings. They do not give in to self-pity—even knowing that rebuilding may take an estimated three years. Rather, they turn to one another and work to clean it up. For example, following the tornado, many of the 240 high school students who found their school destroyed showed up to help clean up the debris. Jon Tompson, the district's superintendent, reflected on the events not by emphasizing the ruin and tragedy but rather by noting the way everyone came together to help one another. He said "Being here, right now, is just tremendous. It just seems like the entire community has come together."[61]

Another example of this speaks to me in the same article from *USA Today,* where a mother tells of how she fought back tears as she pulled up to her 21-year-old daughter's home and saw it in complete ruins. Rushing to the pile of rubble, she began lifting objects and moving them—hoping that she would not find body parts of her dead daughter. Instead, a fire fighter stopped her and told her that he had pulled her daughter to safety before the tornado had hit. She immediately thanked God for her daughter's safety.[62]

Neighbors Helping Neighbors

Even those who have lost loved ones have found comfort in the love and support of their community and surrounding communities. Discussion boards have multiple messages of thoughts and prayers. And many local residents who were not affected are rallying to provide money, food, shelter, and supplies. This week, the American Red Cross teamed up with local news station KWWL to lead the fund raising drive "Neighbors Helping Neighbors," which raised $336, 000 for the victims of the tornado.[63] Additionally, the Salvation Army Disaster Services has served 10,170 meals and food items. 74 staff and volunteers have given more than 620 hours of service.[64]

The USDA Rural Development is also offering housing assistance to victims and providing water to the communities who have had a decline in the water supply. [65]

With all of this outpouring of love and support, how can one not see God's work in all of the debris and shambles? While we might be tempted to at first despair about living in a world where we suffer at the hands of natural disasters beyond our control, much like the young Lewis, the prudence of our faith quickly advises us to turn our eyes to what Lewis later called "the cheerful" side of things. We must look at how God pours out his love and mercy on us to pull us from the dark waters that might easily lead us to the destruction of pessimism and self-pity. And like the crew and community members of the tornado victims, we must also be willing to offer our hands to pull others out from their dark waters.

Finding Purpose

Lewis uses the scene of the Dark Island to show his own journey into Atheism. He creates an allegory so that we might avoid the deep, dark waters of agony that he fell into. Use the following questions to consider the allegory on a more personal level.

What train tunnel leads you to dark waters?

When have you journeyed into dark waters?

What led you seek God's help and mercy?

Who pulled you out?

What was your reaction when you were pulled to safety?

Which of Lewis's advice is most helpful for you? Why?

Finding Scripture

The Calming of the Storm

Lewis named fear as leading him to Atheism. He feared his world because he could not control it. He felt that the universe was a large and oppressing force from which he could not escape. He saw himself as a very little man in a large, cold, and evil space that inflicted pain and suffering upon him. The fear then led him to self-pity and despair from which he felt there was no escape. As mentioned earlier, all of us find ourselves in this predicament from time to time. Jesus's disciples also knew this overwhelming feeling of fear. We are told of such a time in Matthew 8:23-25.

Remember when Jesus takes his disciples out to sea on a boat? While Jesus is sleeping, a violent storm comes upon them and begins to take control of the boat. It is tossed all over and the disciples fear they will be swallowed by the waves. As you can imagine, they felt completely at the mercy of nature and were afraid for their lives. Frantic they run to Jesus—pleading for him to save them from death. Jesus asks them why they are afraid and reprimands them for having little faith. Don't we see ourselves here? Don't we also lose faith in times of peril and become frantic? Jesus reminds us that he controls the elements. God will take care of us in times of need. We must not fear, but trust in him. If we truly believe in him, even death is nothing to fear. For Jesus has conquered it and given us eternal life. But the key is to trust and believe. This is where we often stumble.

Suggested Scripture Reading and Reflections

To further reflect on your own fears and need for faith, read Matthew 8:23-25. Use the following questions to help you find faith.

When are you most like to fear? Why?

When have you run frantically to Jesus for help? What was the result?

What storms do you need Jesus to calm?

How will you find the faith to calm your storm?

Who does Jesus most often send to rescue you? Describe or reflect on one of the times Jesus has rescued you.

When has Jesus helped you rescue someone from a storm? How did you feel?

How did you find the strength?

HEARING GOD'S WILL

REFLECTIONS ON LEWIS'S VOYAGE

When Caspian reaches the World's End, he convinces himself that he is to go to Aslan's country with Reepicheep. He tells his crew that they are to return to Ramandu's Island without him. When Lucy, Edmund, Reepicheep, and the others try to reason with him and help to prudently realize that only Reepicheep is to go on to Aslan's country and that as king it is his duty to return to Narnia—he will hear none of it. In fact, he throws down a ladder in a moment of temper, storms into his cabin and slams the door.

Surely, you must see yourself here. I know I see myself. Don't we all have these moments from time to time? We really know in our hearts what God is calling us to do but we try to convince ourselves that God is calling us to do what **we want to do**. Prudence tells us otherwise, but our own selfish desires argue with prudence and God's whisperings. We create inner turmoil and a foggy confusion. And when others try to point us back to God's path, we sometimes become belligerent and angry.

Lewis describes himself in this manner in *Surprised by Joy*, where he felt his soul stirring with joy throughout his life. But he refused to recognize those longings as his soul's desire to be reunited with God. Instead, he tried to convince himself that they were part of nature and separate from any supreme being. And even when he did finally realize that the stirrings were part of God and God's calling for him—Lewis still explained to himself that was "no possibility of being in a personal relation with him." [66] But God did not give up on Lewis. And eventually, Lewis gave in to God's calling out to him and "chose to open, to unbuckle." It was then that God transformed from what Lewis knew as a "philosophical theorem" to a "living presence who said " 'I am the Lord; 'I am that I am'; 'I am.'"[67] Lewis finally discovered that "God was Reason itself." And finally, giving up the selfish desire "to call [his] soul his own," Lewis took the "absolute leap in the dark" and "gave in." Describing himself as "alone in that room in Magdalen," he "admitted that God was God, and knelt and prayed." Then, he discovered that the "hardness of God is kinder than the softness of men."[68]

Like Caspian, Lewis had his own selfish desire for his destiny. Caspian refused to listen to reason and prudence—being articulated by his crew members and closest friends—in the same way that Lewis had refused to listen to his stirrings, friends' arguments, and the reasoning of some of his most beloved authors, such as Chesterton. He admired them and respected to them, but he would not fully accept them. And, thus, he kept himself from fully embracing joy.

Fortunately, Lewis eventually chooses to listen to and accept reason. He recognizes its presence as God. I believe he chooses to use Caspian to metaphorically depict this moment of his life. For Caspian angrily goes into his cabin alone and slams the door—much like Lewis sat alone in his own room at Magdalen. And there (much like Lewis) alone in the cabin, Caspian finally hears and listens to Aslan. In relaying the event to others, Caspian says "that gold lion's head on the wall spoke to me." Does this not remind you of the "philosophical theorem" that Lewis tells us "stood up" and became a "living presence" and demanded "all"?[69] And this inanimate gold lion also made the same type of demands of Caspian. He told Caspian that he was "to go back. Alone. And at once."[70] There was no other way around it. And Caspian had realized this all along. That is why he was so upset and angry. He was fighting what he really knew deep inside to be prudent, as Lewis had been fighting all along what he knew to really be God.

In his final interview while reflecting on this event and his depiction of it in his autobiography, Lewis said that what he heard God saying to him at that moment was "Put down your gun and we'll talk."[71] While he is obviously being metaphorical here, we get a glimpse of the same kind of anger and hostility Caspian had when he went into his room and slammed the door. And of the same kind of anger and hostility we also take into our rooms when we are resisting God's will for us—even when we have falsely convinced ourselves that we are doing otherwise. Perhaps, in this scene, Lewis is calling us to reflect on our guns and how God is calling us to put them down so that "we can talk."

Personal Ponderings
"The 3-D Approach"

Many of us admit to wanting to do God's will. But often become confused and perplexed in knowing what that is. We say that we are listening, and sometimes we even believe we know what it is, but then find ourselves angry, confused, and upset when we what we thought was God's will doesn't seem to work out as we thought it would. What seems very simple—doing God's will—becomes complex and a source of frustration.

I could say that it was coincidental that the pastor of my parish was talking about this exact same subject this Sunday, but I don't believe it was. Rather, I believe God was helping me to understand this topic in a way that might also help you.

In his homily, our pastor, explained what he called the 3-D approach for coming to understand and know God's will. What he meant by this was a 3-step recursive process that involves Desire, Discernment, and Doing. He says that in order to do God's will we really must desire to do it. And this is true in the above examples of Caspian and Lewis. Both of them found anger, disappointment, and frustration because they were really wanting to follow their own desires than their own. I think this might also be true of ourselves. We say we want to do God's will—but what we really want to do is follow the desires of our own heart. And we trick ourselves into believing these are the same desires of God's will. But they are not.

So, we also must discern if our desires are in fact God's desires. How do we discern this? Prudence and reason often help. We can examine our feelings. Caspian and Lewis were not happy when they were following their own desires. This might also be true of ourselves. If we find ourselves frustrated, angry, and confused, it might be because we are really only convincing ourselves that we are following God's will. Usually, God' will brings true peace and contentment.

If you remember, Caspian and Lewis's friends also voiced reason and prudence on the matter. They later found what their friends told them to also be consistent with what Aslan and God told them. Often times, God speaks to us through others. Listening to our trusted family members and friends may also help us to discern and know God's will.

Lewis and Caspian also both spent time alone in their rooms. I don't think this is coincidental. I have also found that quiet and solitude help me to hear God more clearly. This is where I best pray. And prayer may be the most important part of discernment. For that is where you are able to meet God in a personal and intimate relationship. It allows you to shut out all of the chaos and misleading influences and just listen to what God is whispering in your soul. Prayer will also help you in honestly discerning whether or not you have true peace and contentment in your decision.

Finally, we are called to courageously do what God is calling us to do. It is one thing to desire to do God's will and to know what God's will is, but actually doing it can require a lot of faith. Again, this is where we need prayer and the help of others. We are not required to do it all alone. God promises to walk beside us with the Holy Spirit, our faith community, and our trusted family and friends. Lewis did not change in one night. He spent a lifetime in this recursive relationship of doing God's will. It is not a one-time feat. If we take our Christianity seriously, we realize that the feat is never ending and always changing. And the 3 D's really are essential.

Caspian did not find his calling easy either. Lewis shows him as rather dismal and depressed about what he is called to do. But Lucy encourages him and tells him that he will feel better once he reaches Ramandu's Island. And there is an important lesson for us in this. We may not feel content about doing God's will right away. That peace and contentment might be interrupted by our continued selfish desire to choose our own path. But, if we continue to listen to the voice of God speaking to us in others, and to take courage and heart in that, we will find that peace and contentment. Caspian did eventually find that when he returned to the island. And, Lewis finally found the peace and happiness he had always searched for. Many of his friends described him after his conversion as finally being happy. His melancholy was gone. He had a much more optimistic outlook on life. Perhaps, this 3-D approach might do the same for us.

Finding Purpose

What are your guns that God is asking you to put down?

When have you resisted God's will? What was the result?

When has God stood up and become a living presence to you? How did you react?

When have you convinced yourself that you were truly doing God's will but later discovered it was your own?

Who does God most often speak to you through? How do you know when it is God?

Where can you go to truly be alone with God?

Finding Scripture

Doing God's Will

In Matthew 7, Jesus teaches about how we are to live our lives. In these teachings, we find many moral challenges. One of these challenges involves doing God's will. Here, Jesus tells us that only those who do the will of his father will enter the kingdom. And, so, here we find the reason for the 3D approach to our faith. If we don't, desire, discern, and do God's will, we will not share in his eternal life.

To emphasize and clarify the importance of this teaching, Jesus uses the metaphor of the two houses. One is built on rock—those one who listened to Jesus's teachings and acted on them. The other is built on sand—those who listened but did not act on them. The result, the house built on rock can weather any storm. The other house is completely ruined.

What this metaphor tells me is that Jesus's words are meant to protect me from moral collapse and harm. God wills to protect me from ruin. Jesus's teachings are intended to help me discern and find God's will for me. If I live Jesus's teachings, I will avoid collapse. If I do not find the courage to "do" God's will, I will never know him. I will end up in a pile of wreckage when the spiritual storms come way.

Suggested Scripture Reading and Reflections

Read Matthew 7:21-28, and then use the following questions to further reflect on how God is calling you to do his will.

What does this reading tell you is God's will for you?

What do we need to do to insure that Jesus will know us on the final day?

What rocks are you using to build your house?

Which rocks are missing or cracked?

How will you replace them?

What spiritual storms have you weathered? Which storms are you weathering now?

Which storms are the hardest for you to weather? Why?

How does your foundation help you weather the storms?

Food for the Journey

Reflections on Lewis's Voyage

When the crew finds itself on the island of the beginning of the World's End, they also find a stone table set up with a ready feast. They are tempted to eat but fear that it might lead them into an enchanted sleep. But soon Ramandu, the lady of the island and star at rest, appears and places a bright silver candle on the table. She asks them why they have not eaten and if the table and stone knife looks familiar. Upon closer recognition, Lucy recognizes it as Aslan's table and the stone knife as the knife the White Witch used to kill Aslan. Ramandu explains that the food appears there daily for travelers journeying to the World's End.

Do you recognize the table? Does it not look familiar to you? Perhaps, it reminds you (as it does me) of the altar at Mass. Don't we also find food there prepared and made fresh daily? Does it not also provide nourishment for our journey to the World's End? I believe this might be what Lewis was hinting at in this scene. And the children's fear and doubt about eating it might be his attempt to reflect the doubts believers have about it truly being the body and blood of Christ when Edmund remarks to Ramandu, "I don't mean to be rude. But we have had a lot of queer adventures on this voyage of ours and things aren't always what they seem.... How are we to know?" Don't you hear yourself here as well? Hasn't your faith journey also involved a lot "of queer adventures" causing you to doubt? When you take part in the Eucharist, have you not occasionally wondered if things really are "what they seem?" And maybe secretly asked "How are we to know?" Lewis responds to these questions through Ramandu who replies "You can't know.... You can only believe—or not." [72]

Walter Hooper tells us in his reminiscent essay "Oxford's Bonny Fighter" that Lewis responded to Professor Price's presentation of this quandary by explaining that there are two kinds of Faith: "Faith-A and "Faith-B". Those of Faith-A do not necessarily have a religious faith. As anyone can believe but not act on those beliefs. But those of Faith-B must act with "'trust, or confidence,'" which "involves an attitude of the will, and is more like our confidence in a friend."[73] And in this case, the believer often must trust that what they are being asked to do will be in their best interest—even if it seems dangerous, involves risk, or may be painful. Lewis uses examples such as removing a thorn from a finger, teaching someone to swim, or encouraging someone to climb higher to avoid falling from a ledge as every day examples where this type of trust is required.[74] He argues that this is the same type of trust we must have in God in order to believe. We must accept what we can't know and trust that it will be in our best interest.

This is exactly what Reepicheep decides to do when he drinks from the cup and says to Ramandu, "Lady, I pledge you."[75] Here, at Aslan's table, Lewis shows us what we must also do at Jesus's altar. We must drink from his cup, of his blood, and say "Amen. I believe. I pledge you." We must believe that when eating at Jesus's table we will receive nourishment for our journey to the World's End. And in this act, one of "the sacred paradoxes" that Lewis believes "the human race must not be told too soon," we will find "that to die is to live."[76]

Personal Ponderings

The Little Flower

As I reflect on the two types of faith that Lewis presents here, I find myself overwhelmed with the challenge. Sometimes it is so hard to trust. When life throws us into spiritual, physical, emotional, and financial turmoil, most of us doubt at least a little. We may even ask "God, where are you?" or "Are you even there, God?" At times like this, I find it helpful to look to the heroes of our faith for encouragement. In them I find real-life examples of how to live out Jesus's teachings. They embraced Jesus's message "that to die is to live," as they strengthened their relationship with God and put complete faith in him. Like children, they trusted that God's will would save them and did not falter even while facing hardship and death. One of my favorite saints to look to as a model for believing is Saint Thérèse the Little Flower.

Thérèse, like Lewis, faced the death of her mother at a young age. My heart breaks for both of them. I can't even imagine how difficult that had to be. Unfortunately, some of you have also had to endure this hardship. And while this changed her happy disposition for a while, she turned to her sisters and father to overcome her grief and sadness. But it wasn't until she received the nourishment of Jesus's body and blood at her First Holy Communion that love became her focus. In reflecting on the experience, she describes receiving the Eucharist as "the kiss of love." I wonder what effect the Eucharist might have on us, if we allowed ourselves to look at it in this way—as a "kiss of love"? For Thérèse, it led her to experience a type of ecstasy in her confirmation, which she described as "the sacrament of love."[77]

In *History of a Soul,* Thérèse further demonstrates her ability to trust and believe in God as a child relies on a parent. In discussing her attitude toward prayer she says "... I do as a child who has not learned to read, I just tell our Lord all that I want and he understands."[78] A powerful example of Thérèse's devotion to this type of prayer was demonstrated in 1887, when she was only fourteen. Showing the faith of a child, she prayed fervently for the conversion of a convicted murderer. As his head was placed on a guillotine, he seized the crucifix of a nearby priest and kissed it three times. Thérèse rejoiced in his salvation. This was just one example of what would come to be known as her "little way."[79] Aware of her smallness, Thérèse sought to channel it. She tells us:

> It is impossible for me to grow up, so I must bear with myself such as I am with all my imperfections. But I want to seek out a means of going to heaven by a little way, a way that is very straight, very short and totally new.... I wanted to find an elevator which would raise me to Jesus, for I am too small to climb the rough stairway of perfection. I searched then in the Scriptures for some sign of this elevator, the object of my desires and I read these words coming from the mouth of Eternal Wisdom: 'Whoever is a little one let him come to me.' The elevator which must raise me to heaven is your arms, O Jesus, and for this I have no need to grow up, but rather I have to remain little and become this more and more.[80]

Thérèse, whose feast day is October 1, helps us to remember the importance of being little. Her child-like faith helps us to better understand what Lewis calls Faith-B in our every day struggles. In our own "little way," we can learn to trust God even when it is hard to believe or see what his plan may be. As we seek him in the miracle of the Eucharist, we can find nourishment in his meal of his body and blood and think of it as his "kiss of love" to us—helping us to journey to find him at the World's End.

Finding Purpose

What do you remember about your First Holy Communion?

When did you first feel Jesus's presence in the Eucharist? What did it feel like?

When are you most likely to have doubts about your faith? Why?

When are you most trusting? Why?

How can you work to develop the child-like faith of Thérèse?

Where are you right now on your faith journey? What do you most need Jesus's nourishment for?

Finding Scripture

Food for the Journey

As I read Exodus and listen to the Israelites grumble about their hunger, ungratefully wish they had died in Egypt, and question God's existence, I have to admit ashamedly that I probably would have done the same. I know this because I have also voiced such doubts and complaints in times of adversity. Have not you done the same? Sadly, we have not changed much. And amazingly, God continues to shower us with his love and mercy. Even when we doubt him and utter all kinds of horrid complaints against him, he still continues to feed us and offer us nourishment along our journey.

As the Israelites journeyed out of Egypt and entered the desert of Sin (about 2 and a half months after their exile), they began to panic because they were hungry and had no food. Forgetting the powerful miracles God had performed to ensure their safe exodus from the hands of the pharaoh, they began hurling angry accusations against Moses, Aaron and God. Like us, they gave into despair and doubt. Yet, God sent them a wonderful sweet bread called manna, and the flesh of quail, to nourish them and fill them as they journeyed in the desert. And then when they complained against God again about their thirst, God told Moses to tap his staff on a rock, which brought fresh flowing water for them to drink.

Here, we get a foreshadowing of the nourishment God provided us through Jesus. The manna and quail symbolized the body and blood of Jesus. The fresh flowing water represented the water that would flow from his body when it was pierced with the soldier's sword. Here, we see our baptismal waters to quench our thirst for eternal life.

The Israelites journey in the desert and their angry complaints mirror our own faith journeys and times of doubt. As published literature critic and professor, Lewis surely would have recognized this foreshadowing and symbolism. And I don't think it is too much of a stretch to say that he is calling us to reflect on these journeys in the journey of the crew and the nourishment they receive for their journey to the World's End. I can see and hear myself in the crews' fears and doubts, and I strive to have the courage and faith to drink from the cup as Reepicheep does. Read Exodus 16—17:7, and then use the questions that follow to reflect on your own faith journey and times of doubt, and the nourishment you receive in the body and blood of Jesus.

Suggested Scripture Reading and Reflections

Moses and Aaron helped to lead and guide the Israelites on their journey. On the *Dawn Treader*, Reepicheep often provides wisdom and guidance for the crew when they give into fear or doubt. Who leads you on your journey of faith?

How do you lead others on their journeys of faith?

Describe a time when you lost faith in God. Why did you doubt? How did you feel? How did God rescue you?

How does the Eucharist nourish you on your journey?

Entering God's Kingdom

Reflections on Lewis's Voyage

As I watched Reepicheep ride the great wave over the mountains and vanish into Aslan's kingdom, I wished that I could also have that same kind of enthusiasm and courage in entering God's kingdom. Lewis tells us that Reepicheep was "quivering with happiness." Clearly he was not afraid of leaving his friends and going on alone into another realm where he would live out eternity. He was truly excited. He had achieved the climax of his journey. When I think of my own journey in this way, death doesn't seem quite so scary. For, what if I learned to see my life here as only a journey to God's kingdom? I know this doesn't seem new. We have heard this before. But have you really stopped and pondered the significance of it?

If we think of our earthly lives as only part of a journey, then all of the material aspects of this world become insignificant. They are merely landscape to be briefly enjoyed or obstacles to overcome on the adventure. Looking at our lives in this light, helps us to understand the temporary condition of this world. And then all of our complaints and abuses begin to only seem as temporary challenges that can be overcome. We find hope in knowing it is only temporary and intended to strengthen us for more challenges to come. Also, the material loses its glitter when we see the worldly attractions as also temporary. What is the point in wasting time on things that will not last or matter in the next world? They only become excess baggage and distractions that bog us down as we travel to our ultimate location.

Lewis touches upon this in elaborating Jesus's teaching that it would be difficult for the rich to enter the Kingdom of God. Lewis believes that when Jesus says rich he means it "in every sense—good fortune, health, popularity, and all the things one wants to have." He believes that temptation of all these things is that they "make you feel independent of God, because if you have them you are happy already ... and so you try to rest in a shadowy happiness as if it could last for ever. But God wants to give you a real and eternal happiness." If you rely on these "things" you will never seek it and are doomed to be unhappy as they eventually fail you—and they will because material items do not last. Ask those who have had their homes burn down, their businesses go bankrupt, cars crash, health fail them, and so on. Why must it be this way? Why does God allow these things to happen? As Lewis reminds us, if these things didn't fail, we would "go on relying on them." And while Lewis agrees that this might seem "cruel" and admits that he was once of this same mindset, he has found that it depends on how you perceive your situation in this world. If you see our lives here as "intended simply for our happiness," any inconvenience or hardship becomes unfathomable and unacceptable. But if we see our lives here as a temporary "place of training or correction" to be passed through on our journey to God's kingdom—where the rest of our lives will be lived in oblivion—then all of these hardships don't seem "so bad."

And reflecting on Reepicheep's journey to Aslan's Kingdom, I see that this was his very mindset. He courageously met each obstacle or challenge as part of the adventure of his journey. Keeping his final destination always in sight, nothing came his way ever overwhelmed him. He journeyed with the others valiantly, helping them along the way, but keeping his own location in sight. And thus, it didn't even faze him to learn that he would continue on alone and enter in a different way from the rest of his crew mates. It was just one last feat to embrace before he reached the end of his journey. And isn't this how it might be for us? We journey here together, helping one another along the way, but in the end we will each meet our entrance into God's kingdom differently—and on our own. But this is not to fear. Lewis found "assurance of the New Testament regarding events to come." Shouldn't we as well?

Personal Ponderings

"Another Leg on the Journey"

 Today, as I read the local news, I was struck and inspired by the words of one of the Iowa National Guard's soldiers embarking on his third deployment to the Mid-East in the past six years. In reflecting on his departure, Warrant Officer Al Kakac said "It's just something we do. We're kind of used to it. You don't wear this uniform unless you know it's an eventuality."[87] I couldn't help but smile and think of Reepicheep here. Doesn't Kakac's courage and attitude remind you what Lewis personifies in Reepicheep? Certainly, Kakac and the other soldiers help exemplify how we are to look at our own journeys. Shouldn't we also be so immersed in our Christian faith and doing God's will that we just become "kind of used to it?" And doesn't he sum up our journey to God's Kingdom beautifully? Couldn't being a Christian also be seen as wearing a "uniform" that makes us aware of our own "eventuality" to which we are journeying?

 And Kakac was not alone in his outlook on departure. All of the soldiers shown on the news looked at the journey with optimism. What many of us might see as frightening, dreadful, and insurmountable, they embraced as just part of the adventure of their own unique journeys. For example, Specialist Braden Larsen's remarks on leaving were "I'm just taking it all in stride. Just doing what I'm supposed to do. Do my job and keeping it safe."[88] Others reiterated this sentiment and saw the voyage as giving them a chance to perform the duties they have been trained for. While they were saddened by leaving family behind, like Reepicheep they embraced what they felt called to do—bravely journey to protect and serve others in their calling—knowing they might be nearing God's Kingdom in doing so. The article described these soldiers as traveling on "another leg of their journey." What if we could each embrace each little bump in our day as the same? I wonder how our journeys might change.

Finding Purpose

What is your attitude as you journey to God's Kingdom?

How do you view challenges and obstacles? How might your attitude change if you view these as only part of a journey? As part of an adventure toward God's kingdom?

Who most exemplifies the attitude of Reepicheep and our soldiers in your life? What most inspires you about this person? Why?

Where does this person find his or her strength, hope, and courage?

What could you do to more fully embrace your journey? How can you approach it with more hope and optimism?

Finding Scripture

Letting Go of Our Riches

Reepicheep's journey to God's Kingdom causes me to spend more time pondering Jesus's response to the rich man who knelt before him and asked what he must do to inherit eternal life. Jesus reminded him of the Ten Commandments. And when the man replied that he had been following the commandments since his youth, Jesus challenged him further. He told the man to give away all of his riches to the poor and then to follow him. The man walked away sad because he had many possessions and could not bear to part with them. While those of us who are not wealthy might be quick to criticize this man, we might remember that Lewis considered all of our good fortunes to be riches. And perhaps, if we were honest with ourselves, we might see ourselves in this man. Do we give up all that we have to follow Jesus? Or do we only give up enough to say we do—but still keep ourselves comfortable? Do we place God above all of our earthly possessions?

That is really what Jesus is challenging us with here—to place all of our happiness and trust in God on a second by second basis. If we really did this, we might all be homeless and happy in this homelessness. I doubt that many of us fully embrace this. Jesus even admitted to the crowd that this type of faith was impossible for humans—but not for God. And that is where we find the key—God. We must learn to pray for the strength and courage to embrace God's will on a second by second basis without looking too far ahead at what will come. As difficult as it may be, Jesus calls us to journey onward accepting our tasks and challenges with the optimism that we will eventually enter in his kingdom at the end of our journey—where Jesus tells us we will have much more than this world could ever offer us—and there it will be for eternity. To spend some time pondering what Jesus's teachings are asking of you, read Mark 10:17-31 and reflect on the questions that follow.

Suggested Scripture Reading and Reflections

Why is it so hard for us to let go of our earthly possessions?

What possessions would be the hardest for you to part with? Why?

How do these possessions keep you from embarking on your journey?

How might they keep you out of God's Kingdom?

What can you do to live second by second placing your trust only in God?

Section Two: Tales of Temperance

> There is a difference between doing some particular just or temperate action and being a just or temperate man.[1]

Negating the Negative

Reflections on Lewis's Voyage

As mentioned in section one, Eustace did not begin the voyage as the most positive shipmate. In fact, he was horribly negative and as a result difficult to tolerate. His constant complaints made it very almost unbearable to be in his presence. Certainly, we have all encountered such individuals in our families, work places, schools, and communities. Dealing with them is never easy—and most of us can probably remember times when we have also been like Eustace. By helping us to remember and reflect on these times, Lewis also presents an attitude that might help us respond more positively in these encounters. Through Lucy, Lewis suggests that instead of responding with criticism, ridicule, and disdain that we offer empathy and support—as difficult as that may be.

If you recall, when the children begin their voyage, Eustace suffers from seasickness. Rather disgusted with Eustace's response to any kind of help, Edmund surmises "... I don't think we can do anything for him. It only makes him worse if you try to be nice to him."[2] Can you not think of times when this was also your response after receiving complaint and criticism to your attempts of help? Most of us become frustrated and use the negative response as an excuse for continuing to offer help. As a result, the person we were trying to help does not get the help needed and may reside in his negative mind set. Instead, Lucy listens to her "conscience" which had begun to "smote her" and says "I think I really must go and see Eustace. Seasickness is horrid, you know."[3] Discovering that Caspian has her cordial, she decides to use it to cure Eustace's seasickness. Caspian (not very empathetically) voices our own question: Should it "be wasted on a thing like seasickness?"[4] Lucy responds "It'll only take a drop."[5]

And here we get at the heart of temperance. Caspian might think himself being temperate in wondering about when and how the cordial should be used. And Edmund might also find himself temperate in considering how to best spend his time and offer his services. We often convince ourselves we are being temperate with similar responses. But, Lucy shows us that temperance might be more of an empathetic response to all in need—regardless of how they respond to us and treat us. And additionally, she does not lecture or impose her principles upon Edmund or Caspian. She merely takes it upon herself to treat and care for Eustace—despite his ungrateful growl: "Oh, go away and leave me alone."[6]

What is the result? Lucy's compassionate attitude convinces Eustace to drink the potion, and he feels well. Additionally, he begins to see that some people do care and sees how to also act in kindness. We get a glimpse of the beginning of Eustace's awareness of this when he writes in his journal: "I always try to consider others whether they are nice to me or not."[7] While the irony here is that Eustace rarely considers others, the point might be that Eustace is beginning to become aware that he *should* consider others. And perhaps his awareness is the result of Lucy's continued care and empathy for him. For after giving him the cordial, Eustace's diary reveals that she also was the only one who visited him in his cabin and also offered him her water when he was thirsty.

Through Lucy, Lewis demonstrates the attitude of temperance. He shows that it is more about a way of living and thinking than acts of abstaining. He directly comments on this in his book *Christian Behaviour* when he explains that the "whole point" of temperance is "abstaining, for a good reason, from something which [one] does *not* condemn and which [one] likes to see other people enjoying."[8]

PERSONAL PONDERINGS

Interestingly, I believe many would look at Lucy's actions toward Eustace as admirable—but not very bright. They would look at the situation as Edmund and Caspian had—wasteful of the cordial and time. Resources should be saved for situations of greater value and better outcome. Eustace was not worth the time, effort or cordial. And in essence, this attitude spreads the negativity that Eustace embodies—yet this attitude is more easily hidden and often cloaked in progressivism.

The attitude I speak of is not hard to find. In fact, just this morning I found it while reading of Professor Richard Lynn's contentions that people who believe in God have lower IQs.[9] His study attempts to prove that as children develop they become more intelligent and question God's existence. Those who do not question God and continue to believe simply are retarded in their intellectual development.[10] As preposterous as this may sound to some of us, it does present a prevalent trend and attitude that attempts to excuse us from our moral obligations. By negating God's existence, we excuse ourselves from the challenges he presents us with. If we don't believe in God, we don't need to bother with what may be difficult to understand or the challenges that understanding might present. It is much easier to respond with the logic of Edmund and Caspian than with the temperance of Lucy.

Fortunately, Lynn's study is not being blindly accepted as fact. Many are finding its conclusions too simple. And some critics like

Dr. David Hardman, principal lecturer in learning development at London Metropolitan University, are realizing that "There is evidence from other domains that higher levels of intelligence are associated with a greater ability - or perhaps willingness - to question and overturn strongly felt institutions."[11]

As I have noted previously, Lewis also struggled with questions that Lynn poses. In fact, for many years, he also found it preposterous to believe in religion. He found himself to be intellectually above it. But as he grew in spiritual maturity, he reached the same conclusion as Saint Paul. "Christ never meant that we were to remain children in intelligence: on the contrary, He told us to be not 'as harmless as doves,' but also 'as wise as serpents.' He wants a child's heart, but a grown-up's head." And then Lewis leaves us with a warning, "If you are thinking of becoming a Christian, I warn you; you are embarking on something which is going to take the whole of you, brains and all.... a Christian will soon find his intelligence being sharpened.[12]"

In offering an authentic example of this and applying it to tolerance, Lewis turns our attention to charity. While conceding that in giving to charity we must also need to intelligently discover where and how our donations are applied,[13] he also refused to accept the current negative notion that we should not give to the poor because they will never learn to provide for themselves. While he agreed that we should encourage citizens to care for themselves, it does not excuse us from giving. And in discerning how much we should give, he found the only "safe rule" to be: "more than we can spare."[14]

Those, like Lynn, who might see these moral and religious views of temperance unintelligent, could actually be responding to their own discomforts with the questions and challenges that religion often poses. And in their discomfort, are they negatively labeling those of us who embrace and grapple with those questions? How should we respond? Like Lucy, we must reach out to them with understanding, empathy, kindness—and perhaps prayer. Rather than lecturing or preaching, we must allow our actions to model our beliefs. How much should we offer them? According to Lewis, "more than we can spare."

Finding Purpose

When have you helped someone who was not appreciative? How did you respond to his or her complaints and criticisms? What was the result?

Why is it so difficult to respond as Lucy did?

How can you be more temperate in your attitude and actions?

When we think of charity, we often think of giving money to the poor. But, charity also involves serving others with our talents and time. How well do you meet the challenge to "give more than you can spare"?

What excuses do you create to convince yourself that you give enough?

Finding Scripture

Chapters 24 and 25 of Matthew give us much to ponder about temperance. They teach us that we must be prepared for Jesus's coming for he will come with no warning. What does it mean to be prepared? The parables offered here tell us to be actively serving God by serving others with the talents he has given us. Those who are not using the talents they have been given will be cast into darkness. Those who have not remained awake with their lamps burning will find closed doors. Those who do not feed the hungry, give drink to the thirsty, clothe the naked, care for the sick, and visit the prisoners will suffer eternal punishment. In these parables, we also reach the same conclusion as Lewis—we must give more than we can spare.

We also realize that temperance is not only about giving up pleasures; temperance calls us to willingly use the talents we have been given to serve others. Hoarding them or wasting them on our own pleasures will lead us to eternal anguish and isolation from God.

Suggested Scripture Reading and Reflections

Read Chapters 24 and 25 of Matthew. Then use the following questions for reflection and discussion.

Which of the parables leaves you with the most questions? Why?

Which of the parables gives you the most challenge? Why?

What common theme runs through all of the parables?

How do the parables speak to you about temperance?

Based on these chapters and the scene presented from *The Voyage of the Dawn Treader,* how would you define temperance?

Troubled with Treasure

Reflections on Lewis's Voyage

Not surprisingly, Eustace's selfish and negative attitude led him into much mischief when the crew finally reached an island. While his fellow shipmates worked diligently to repair the ship and replenish their food and water stores, he slipped away to avoid work and to explore. And in his explorations, he stumbled upon a deceased dragon and its treasure. Not having given much thought to treasure before, Eustace greedily considered the pleasures it might bring him and how on this island he could avoid paying any tax. He greedily filled his clothing with as much of the treasure as he could carry—including a diamond bracelet which he slid onto his arm past his elbow. He then, ironically, nestled himself in the treasure and fell asleep.

What was the result? As you might suspect, Eustace's slumber in the treasure symbolized a spiritual slumber that further separated him from others. In awakening, Eustace soon discovered that "sleeping on a dragon's hoard with greedy, dragonish thoughts in his heart, he had become a dragon himself."[15] And the bracelet that he had slid on to his arm served as a painful reminder. It caused "a throbbing bulge on each side" of his arm. And even his dragon teeth "could not get it off."[16] And even more painfully, in wanting to rejoin his friends and shipmates, "he realized that he was a monster cut off from the whole human race."[17] And then, he finally began a self-introspection where he wondered about his past treatment of others.

Through Eustace, I have to wonder if Lewis isn't remembering his own struggles before he re-found his Christian faith. While he never hoarded treasure, he did spend much of his time buried and consumed in treasures of literature. And in his autobiography *Surprised by Joy*, he describes the moment of when he began his descent into literary priggishness as preceded by his befriending two boys from "the Dragon School at Oxford."[18] Could it be that Lewis was using Eustace to remember those times of his life? Did he see himself as a dragon—acting like a monster, cut off from others? He does admit that at that time in his boyhood his "social struggle ... was the absorbing preoccupation."[19] This also seems to be the case for Eustace.

And so Lewis seems to be presenting us with a valuable lesson here: "The World will lead you only to Hell."[20] In other words, if you immerse yourself in the pleasures of this world and become self-absorbed in those pleasures, you may become a dragon—a monster—isolated from God and others. And in your isolation, your physical, worldly treasure will cause you great pain and anguish.

Personal Ponderings

Recent weather events this past spring have caused many to realize that the treasures we build here on earth are temporary. What we have today, may be gone tomorrow. News videos, photos, and interviews of those who have lost their homes in the Midwest flooding show homes floating and stuck up against bridges, furniture sailing, and cars completely immerged. There is really no good or easy explanation for tragedies of this magnitude. People have found themselves homeless. And we have all been reminded that we do not have the control over our lives that we try to convince ourselves we have.

Yet the videos, photos, and interviews also show that while earthly treasures may come and go—love does not. As family and friends helped each other sandbag and clean up the damage, we discovered that love binds us together as family and community in even the most difficult times. And in that love, we find God. He does not abandon us. He walks beside us and reminds us that we are not alone. While Eustace may have found treasure and Lewis intellectual social status—they also found themselves very isolated and alone. In order to find true happiness, they needed to let go of their worldly and selfish obsessions. And when they did, they found love, community, and happiness. They discovered that treasure could not provide love and happiness. And in that sense, the floods have not really been tragedies at all. Rather, they have reminded us that we cannot find happiness in the treasures we store here on earth. True happiness resides in the love and support we provide one another.

Finding Purpose

When have you greedily hoarded your treasure? Why? What was the result?

When have you lost a prized possession? How did you react?

Where do you find true happiness?

What could you do to remind yourself each day that happiness cannot be found in treasure?

Finding Scripture

There may be no more humbling Scripture passage to teach us temperance than The Sermon on the Mount. As we read Jesus's words, we find no special recognition for having a high social status. Our house and vehicle do not turn heads. The grades our children are receiving and the positions they are playing in sports do not matter. Nor, do we get extra bonus points for dressing nice or for having sound investments or retirement plans. Here, we hear the exact opposite of what popular media and society preach to us. The poor in spirit, those who mourn, the unpopular and meek, those seeking justice and showing mercy, the pure of heart and peacemakers, and those suffering from persecution are praised, acknowledged, and rewarded with God's kingdom.

I am afraid that most of us will struggle in fitting into these descriptions and categories. Why? We have fallen prey to a myth that promises happiness in worldly values and possessions. As hard as we may have tried to resist this, we have failed miserably. Sure, we have times where we think of others and fight for justice. And we may have had times of mourning or been a peacemaker. But can we honestly say that any of these descriptions truly describe us on a daily basis? Unless we are Mother Teresa, it is doubtful.

Yet this is how we will be measured. This is what God expects from us. We must learn to separate ourselves from the messages of this world and to temper ourselves with the teachings of Christ. And how will we know when we are achieving this? Jesus says that we will know when the people of this world hurl accusations against us and insult us. While that may not sound like much of a reward—and here on earth it would not be—we are promised the reward of **eternal** happiness.

To reflect further on what Jesus is asking of us, read Mathew 5:1-12. Then use the following questions for further discussion and pondering.

Suggested Scripture Reading and Reflections

To be "poor in spirit" means to place your confidence in God rather than worldly possessions. Why is this so difficult for us?

Which of the beatitudes do you struggle with most? Why?

What do the beatitudes teach you about temperance?

It is so easy to fall prey to the messages of this world. What could you do to be more mindful of their influence on you?

What could you do to be more mindful of the beatitudes in your daily choices and actions?

Facing God

Reflections on Lewis's Voyage

When I listened to Eustace tell Edmund his story about meeting Aslan, I found myself reflecting on the sacraments of baptism and reconciliation. Remember how Eustace tells of Aslan leading him to a round marble bath with bubbling water? And then tells Eustace to undress and bathe in the bubbling waters? Doesn't this remind you of being dressed in new, white clothes as we were bathed in Jesus's baptismal waters? And it is interesting that the waters reveal that Eustace has more layers of scales to be scraped off. This reminds me of our many layers of sinful scales. And like us, Eustace finds that he cannot remove them alone. Aslan tells him "'You will have to let me undress you.'"[21] This caused me to reflect on my own dependence on God to remove my layers of sin. I cannot remove them alone. Only the Sacrament of Reconciliation can completely remove my sinful layers. And, like Eustace, I have also found it to be painful at times—but also as Eustace explained "perfectly delicious"[22] once I started swimming and splashing in the cleansing waters. Like Eustace, I have found the waters to take away my pain and suffering. Haven't you also found and felt the same?

Eustace also tells us that Aslan dressed him in "new clothes."[23] And in those new clothes, Eustace finds Edmund and tells him his story as a changed boy. At the end of the tale, he says "I'd like to apologize. I'm afraid I've been pretty beastly."[24] And of course, this parallels the penance we must perform after we are forgiven. We must say "sorry" to those we have hurt with our sinful and "beastly" ways. We must stop being dragons.

This scene also reminded me of Lewis's undressing. Like Eustace followed Aslan, Lewis's curiosity led him to follow God into the region of Awe. And once there, he found that he had in following been only asking " 'What is it?' " He had not asked "'Who is the desired?'"[25] With that realization, he discovered that God was not like him "clothed in the senses."[26] To fully meet the "naked Other" buried within himself, he had to disrobe and bring his philosophy together with his life. He needed to temper his questions. And in that realization, like Eustace he found himself faced with a choice. Lewis, finding himself clothed in "some stiff clothing," knew that he could "unbuckle the armor or keep it on."[27] Like Eustace, he decided to remove his clothing found that he "rather disliked the feeling,"[28] but he soon found that "the hardness of God is kinder than the softness of men, and His compulsion is our liberation."[29] In meeting God, Lewis finally found himself freed from his pessimism and negativity. Could he have been visually depicting this undressing, meeting with God, and new found freedom through Eustace? I think he might.

PERSONAL PONDERINGS

Eustace's journey out of selfishness and spiritual awakening reminds of Oscar Wilde's tale of "The Selfish Giant." Do you remember the mean and selfish Giant who would not let anyone play in his garden? When children would climb over the wall to play in his garden, he would holler at them and tell them to leave. Scared of his angry appearance and large size, the children would run off in fright. The giant's garden was beautiful and plentiful, but he refused to share it. Like Eustace he was selfish and consumed with negative thoughts; he saw the children as a nuisance and as a threat to his garden. Rather than looking at their visiting as a chance to share and enjoy the garden with others, as an opportunity for friendship, the giant consumed himself with angry and selfish energy, which he then projected on to those who tried to enter the garden. Thus, the wall became a metaphorical parallel for the wall of selfishness that he had built around his heart. As a result, his garden only knew winter—never spring. (Perhaps, this is where Lewis found his inspiration for his book *The Lion, The Witch and the Wardrobe*. Remember how the White Witch made Narnia always winter and never spring?)

Eventually, the Giant realized that when the children come over the wall they bring Spring to the parts of the garden they play in. Like Eustace, he then began to see the beast that he had become. But it is not until he is visited by a little boy with wounds in his hands (Christ) that he learns the value of unselfish giving. With this lesson, he finally tears down his wall of sin and selfishness. Jesus helps the Giant to remove the remaining stones of his wall. His heart is then cleansed and left naked and unprotected to be shared with others. The Giant was helped to remove his last stubborn, sinful barriers, as Aslan helped Eustace remove his final layers of sinful scales and we are helped to cleanse ourselves of sin in the Sacrament of Reconciliation. Both stories show us that we cannot go it alone. We need the help of others and God to find true and lasting happiness. While our initial temptations might be toward pleasing and protecting ourselves, these stories show that we should resist that urge and instead reach out to God and others.

Finding Purpose

When might others have seen you as a dragon or selfish Giant? Why?

When are you most likely to be selfish, negative or angry toward others?

What scales do you need help removing?

What walls do you need to tear down?

How will you seek help to remove the scales and tear down the wall?

Finding Scripture

In reading the Psalms, I am often struck by the commonality between the faithful followers of the past and the faithful of today. The voices in the psalms speak of the same struggles, challenges, and delights that we have. Thus, in reading them, we find reassurance that we are not alone. Others struggled, suffered, rejoiced, and also found refuge in God. In Psalm 32, we hear from someone who, like us, also struggled with sin and suffering. The writer tells us that like Eustace, Lewis, and us, he or she attempted to deny his selfish and sinful ways. But in refusing to face them and take them to God, the writer only found suffering and anguish. Not until he or she faced God and let go of his or her sinful ways did the writer find relief and happiness. Thus, the writer counsels us to also find temperance by letting go of our selfishness and turning to God in love and trust.

Read Psalm 32 and then reflect on the questions that follow.

Suggested Scripture Reading and Reflections

In which verse did you most relate to the writer? Why?

The writer says that he suffered and found great distress when he kept his sins from God. When have you also felt this type of suffering?

Why is it so difficult to face God? What keeps us from him, even when we know we can only find love and happiness with him?

What counsel does the writer give us? How can you best apply it to find temperance in your life?

Conquering Curiosity

Reflections on Lewis's Voyage

In *Christian Behaviour*, C.S. Lewis names pride "the great sin"[30] because he believes that it was through this sin "that the devil became the devil."[31] He also tells us that this sin leads to "every other vice."[32] He calls it the "complete anti-God state of mind."[33] While he spends great length describing the nature and qualities of the sin, I think his finding it a sin stemming out of competition most applies to Lucy's temptations and fall while browsing through the magician's book of spells.

If you remember, while looking through the pages of the spell book, Lucy finds a spell that would let her know what her friends thought of her. Unable to temper her curiosity and seeking knowledge that was not originally intended for her to have, she recites the spell and listens in on a previous conversation that her friends had about her. The spell allows her to hear what they said on one occasion when she was not around. While listening in, she hears some unpleasant comments that were made about her. As a result, she becomes angry and sheds tears, as she wonders about the rest of her friends' loyalty. The knowledge only leads to unhappiness.

How does this relate to competitiveness? It reveals our tendency to want to be the most liked, the cleverest, the most popular. And in seeking this prestige, we also become overly curious and concerned about what others think of us and say about us when we are not around. What is the result? Lucy shows us. Our pride only leads to unhappiness and discontent. To find true happiness, we must let go of our pride. We must learn to let go of our competitive nature and temper our curiosity—for most of the time the knowledge we gain from our pride is false and misinterpreted.

Aslan helps Lucy to realize that in eavesdropping on her friends, she "misjudged" her friend by failing to realize that she said what she did because "She was weak" and "afraid of the other girl."[34] Aslan reassures Lucy that her friend really does love her and did not mean what she said. Unfortunately, Lucy finds herself unable to erase the conversation from her memory. And she fears that she may have ruined their friendship by listening in on something she was not intended to hear. Perhaps, this is lesson for us as well. Sometimes, ignorance is bliss. Pridefully seeking knowledge not intended us may only cause us misery.

Personal Ponderings

Lucy's plight raises the controversy that has spilled into almost all literature in some shape or form. Was Eve wrong in seeking the knowledge from the forbidden tree in the Garden of Eden? Was God cruel and controlling in forbidding Adam and Eve from eating from the tree of knowledge? John Milton raised these questions in *Paradise Lost* and portrayed a somewhat cold and unfeeling God. Herman Melville also presented this view in *Moby Dick* through Ahab's vengeful journey to kill the great white whale, which symbolically represented God. Nathaniel Hawthorne did the same in his short story *Rapaccinni's Daughter,* where a cold and unfeeling father poisons his daughter and keeps her in a garden in an attempt to protect her. As a result, she dies. More recently, novelist Phillip Pullman raised these controversial questions again with his *Dark Materials* series where Lyra repeats the fall, and it is presented as good and a natural process of maturation. He openly admits that his story is intended as a contrast to Lewis's *Narnia* series where Pullman believes Lewis shows maturing as evil and sinful.[35]

Apparently these are questions that rest at the consciousness of humanity? So how are we intended to view the Creation story? Personally, I agree with Lewis. I believe that Eve's inability to resist the temptation of Satan represented the sin of pride. Eve (and Adam) desired to be as great as God. And thus they became "anti-God." In seeking a knowledge that God knew they were not ready for they thwarted the natural process of maturation. God gave them a free will—although he had advised them not to eat from the tree. He did not remove the tree because that would be taking away free will. Rather, he advised them, and they arrogantly chose to disregard God's advice. They ate because of the prideful and competitive nature to be like God. Like Lucy they yielded to their curiosity that stemmed from a desire to know what they were not intended to know. And as a result, they misjudged the situation and God.

Does this make God unfeeling and uncaring? I don't think so. While Pullman may see the story and religion as trying to thwart maturation and prevent knowledge, I see the story as showing the dangers of trying to speed up the process of maturation. We will never know when we would have been ready for the knowledge of good and evil—because like Lucy we sought it out before we were ready. Was God always going to keep us from that knowledge so he could control us? As Aslan reminds Lucy "one is never told what would have happened." But the fact that the tree was placed in the garden leads me to believe that we would have eventually been led to the knowledge when we had matured enough to judge it and use it correctly. Just as Lucy would have eventually found out what her friends really thought of her through a natural course of events—and thus interpreted them accurately.

Pullman brings back the argument of the Romantics best represented in William Blake's contrasting poems "The Tiger" and "The Lion." Should we educate our children at an early age about social issues and risk a loss of innocence? Is ignorance really bliss? According to Lewis, we don't have to choose. By following a natural progression of maturation, Lewis shows that we gain the knowledge we need with God by our side—as Aslan told Lucy "I have been here all the time"[36]—and in that progression we will not misjudge. Lucy finds these lessons in Narnia. While Pullman criticizes Lewis at not allowing the grown children to return to Narnia once they mature, I believe he fails to recognize that their inability to return is not intended to be punitive or deny knowledge. Rather, as Aslan explains it at the end of *The Voyage of the Dawn Treader,* the children will take the knowledge they found in Narnia into their own world and learn to know Aslan by "another name"[37]—Jesus. Thus, knowledge is not denied us but gradually given to us through our own discoveries as we are ready for it.

Finding Purpose

When have you sought out knowledge that you shouldn't have?

What was the result?

When are you most tempted with curiosity?

How can you temper this curiosity?

How can you be more patient in your own spiritual maturing?

Finding Scripture

In Matthew 13, we are also called to reflect on the gift of knowledge. He explains it to us in the Parable of the Sower. In the parable, we see seed sowed on different types of paths and in different conditions. Afterwards, the disciples question him about his use of parables in teaching. There, Jesus explains the parable and his reasoning for using parables. His words reveal that knowledge is freely given to us but we must also be open to it and be willing to act on the knowledge with wisdom and temperance. For example, Jesus explains that some hear and see what his words mean but allow the anxiety and lure of this world to choke out the world and fruit that it might bear. Thus, temperance seems to be essential to helping us understand and live out the word of God.

Suggested Scripture Reading and Reflections

After reading Matthew 13: 1-23, use the following questions to reflect on how you receive the Word of God in your life.

How does God reveal himself to you?

How can you be sure to see and hear God's Word in your life?

How can you make sure that your soil is fertile and bears fruit?

What weeds do you need to prune so that you might bear fruit?

Adam and Eve ate from the tree too soon, before the fruit was ready for them, how can we avoid making the same mistake?

Loving Ourselves as We Are

Reflections on Lewis's Voyage

Lewis gives us another lesson about pride while Lucy is looking through the book of spells. In addition to being tempted to know what she was not intended to know, Lucy is also tempted with the ability to change her appearance to be more beautiful than Susan. As Lucy encounters a spell that causes her to imagine herself as being prettier than Susan, we again find that pride is linked with our competitive nature, as we discover that Lucy has always compared herself to Susan and seen Susan as the more attractive and favorite of the daughters. Additionally, Lucy sees herself becoming a ruler and in control of others because she is beautiful. Fortunately, before Lucy gets too carried away and recites the spell, she sees the face of Aslan staring into her own.

Lewis teaches us much here. He shows us our own false, prideful comparisons where we measure ourselves less than others. And then as result of the comparisons, convince ourselves that if we change our appearance we will also be more popular, more powerful, and loved more. This scene provides us with a necessary chance to reflect on how we are measuring and valuing ourselves. And in reading this scene, most of us probably felt and understood Lewis's shove for us to do so.

But, there is more to the shove than seeing ourselves here. The lesson is more than learning to love ourselves as we are. I believe the key to this lesson might be found in the fact that Lucy would have recited the spell had she not seen Aslan staring her in the face. I find this to mean that we can only find a healthy self image by seeing God's image in our own, looking back at us. And in order to see God, we must be humble. For in knowing God, we will find a being superior to ourselves. This requires us to look up. And as long as you are "looking down, you can't see something that's above you"—or perhaps within you.[38]

In reflecting on our prideful natures to always strive to be better than others, Lewis confesses "I wish I had got a bit further with humility myself." For then he would able to give us more guidance on "taking the fancy-dress off—getting rid of the false self, with all its 'Look at me' and 'Aren't I a good boy?'"[39] For Lewis believed that only in taking off the fancy dress could we ever get to know God and realize that that it is "all the silly nonsense about [our] dignity which has made [us] restless and unhappy."[40] There we find a relationship with the one who created us: a relationship that we can only begin by taking off all of our false and prideful appearances that keep us from seeing him in ourselves and always before us. Only in removing all of our glitter, glamour, and makeup, can we look in the mirror and find God staring back at us. To do this, Lewis tells us "The first step is to realize that one is proud.... If you think you're not conceited, it means you are very conceited indeed."[41]

Personal Ponderings

What is interesting and tricky about the lesson to love yourself as you are is that you would not immediately see it as in conflict with secular teaching. Many of the commercials tell you to take time for yourself and to pamper yourself. Buy some new shoes, a new dress, or the pair of jeans that will make everyone take notice. They convince you that in the midst of this chaotic and demanding world, you must take time out for your own needs. Go have fun with the girls. Enjoy a night out with the guys. Of course this fun is usually linked to indulging in an alcoholic beverage, cigarette, or a night out gambling. The problem is that this sense of self and happiness promotes materialism and narcissism.

And even when the message seems to be well intended, such as in targeting diseases that result from not loving oneself, such as anorexia, bulimia, and alcoholism, many messengers still keep the focus on the needs of this world. Thus, many seeking treatment fail to heal. Often, those seeking help find themselves replacing one bad habit with another because they seek happiness in another worldly source that will, predictably, fail them. To find true happiness, we need to see the image of God within ourselves.

And perhaps this gets at the heart of the message, which Lewis brings to our attention. One cannot really love himself or herself and have a healthy self-image without coming to know God. And even knowing God can be tricky. For as many of us have witnessed, many Christian people who claim to know and love God are still eaten up by pride. They go to church and help others. In fact, they may even see themselves as very religious. But as Lewis points out, this is the problem. In all of their Christian behavior and charitable works, they are "imagining how He approves of them and thinks them far better than ordinary people."[42] In this case, Lewis finds them "worshipping an imaginary God."[43] Lewis calls this a "death trap" as he reminds us of Jesus's warning that some people would "preach about Him and cast out devils in His name, only to be told at the end of the world that He had never known them."[44] What Lewis is proposing here is that Jesus won't know us because we have never really taken the time to see him. We only know a false appearance of ourselves. And in hiding behind our false appearances we have never seen God's face. We were too preoccupied with seeing our outward appearances and acts in the mirror to see God's appearance looking back at us in the faces of our fellow community members. Had we seen God, we might have had a more accurate measure of ourselves in the large scheme of things and found a humble relationship with others and our God.

This is where the secular messages fail. They fail to show us that learning to love ourselves means learning to love others and God as we love ourselves. They fail to show that in giving to others and listening to others we are also giving to ourselves and listening to ourselves. They also fail to depict how seeking happiness in the material pleasures of this world may lead us to eternal unhappiness as we inaccurately measure our value and place in this world and God's kingdom.

So what does a humble person look like? Lewis says this person might surprise you. He is not necessarily a person dressed poorly and constantly berating him or herself. Rather, the humble person is likely to be pleasant, intelligent, enjoying life, and eager to listen to you. He won't be preaching about humility or thinking about himself at all. In fact, you will likely wish you were like him or her because he or she is so happy.[45] And my guess is that you will never see this type of person in an ad or presented positively by secular media.

Finding Purpose

Which secular messages about self have you been most influenced by?

How can you be more aware of the influences of this world?

According to Lewis, a humble person is a good listener. How can you be a better listener?

In what ways have you been prideful?

How can you find the humility to see God looking you in the face?

How can the sacraments help you to grow in humility?

Finding Scripture

In Scripture, we constantly find the Pharisees and Sadducees trying to trip up Jesus with their questions. In their pride, they resented that someone was getting more attention than them. And, they resented that Jesus was calling many of their actions into question. Rather than looking at Jesus's teachings as opportunities to change and grow closer to God, their pride saw Jesus as competition.

One of these occasions is told of in Matthew 23 when one of the scholars of law questioned Jesus about which of the laws is the greatest. While this question was intended to trap Jesus, it provided us with the greatest lesson on self love. Jesus responds that we should first love the Lord with our whole heart, soul, and mind. And then we should love our neighbor as our self. And here is the lesson, if we truly love God, we will be loving ourself because God is within us. We are created in his image. Thus, loving ourself does not become an issue unless we are lacking in our love of God. Also, if we are truly loving God, we will also be loving others, as God is also present in them. Thus, truly loving God will naturally bring about a love of self and others.

Suggested Scripture Reading and Reflections

After reading Matthew 22: 34-40, use the following questions to reflect on how you can better love yourself.

How do you see yourself? How should you see yourself?

How does this Scripture call the way you see yourself into question?

How can you love God with your whole heart, soul, and mind?

How can you better love your neighbor as yourself?

Seeing Others' Suffering

Reflections on Lewis's Voyage

When Ramandu tells Caspian that leading his crew to east to the end of world would break the enchantment of the three sleeping Lords, he first thinks of his weary crew—even though he greatly desires to sail to the world's end. As a thoughtful and temperate leader, he considers the needs and wishes of his crew before his own. Realizing that they did not originally agree to sail to the world's end and that the voyage has already been long and difficult, he does not commit them to any further voyage. He tells Ramandu "They're brave fellows, but I see signs that some of them are weary of the voyage and long to have our prow pointing to Narnia. I don't think I should take them without their knowledge and consent."[46] And then he also thinks of the needs of Lord Rhoop who he describes as "a broken man."[47]

Lewis gives us a chance to reflect on our leadership skills here. In working toward temperance, do we put the needs of others before our own? Are we able to see the needs of others under our care before our own needs? Like us, Lewis also found this challenging. As I have noted previously in the book, he often worried over his own finances. But, like Caspian, he saw the need to meet the needs of others under his care first.

I think one strong example of this was when Lewis kept his promise to his friend Paddy Moore and took care of Paddy Moore's mother—Mrs. Moore. While Warren tells us that Mrs. Moore was insufferable, demanding, and much different from C.S. Lewis in nature and interests, C.S. Lewis continued to care for her and live under what Warren called the "autocracy of Mrs. Moore ... that developed into a stifling tyranny."[48] In fact, Lewis continued to take care of Mrs. Moore as his "servitude was made more burdensome" with

Mrs. Moore's "senility and invalidism."⁴⁹ Yet, Lewis never complained, and he continued to put her needs above his own, as he also taught at Oxford and continued to write and publish.

Warren also tells us that Lewis's empathy for others and desire to put their needs above his own reached far beyond his care for Mrs. Moore. He says that while the "total of his benefactions will never be known," C.S. Lewis's had "in an extraordinary degree the deeper charity that can perhaps best be described as a universal and sympathetic neighborliness to all and sundry, strangers as well as acquaintances."⁵⁰ He then goes on to tell of two examples. On one occasion, while deeply involved in his writing, he heard mention of a stranger who was ill and stranded in a field "some distance away."⁵¹ Hearing of the man, C.S. Lewis casually remarked " 'poor devil' " and continued on with his writing. Yet, not long after, jumped up, reprimanded himself for his sin of selfishness and said " 'I have shown myself lacking in all charity.' "⁵² He then sought out the man, brought him back to the house, listened to the man's story and took care of his needs until the man was well.

On another occasion, Warren tell us that C.S. Lewis met a "tramp" who knew quite a bit about poetry. As a gesture of kindness, C.S. Lewis gave the man an ample supply of beer and one of his personal anthologies of verse and poetry.⁵³

His stepson, David Gresham, also recently mentioned Lewis' charitable offerings in an interview with CBN. In remembering his stepfather, he shared that Lewis made it a priority to give 2/3 of his royalties to charity. He also told of a time when a homeless man approached C.S. Lewis begging for change. Lewis immediately reached into his pockets and gave the man all that he had. When told by his friends that the man would likely spend the money on beer, Lewis shrugged his shoulders and admitted that he would have probably spent the money in the same manner.⁵⁴

How did Lewis find the strength to put the needs of others above his own? I am sure that it was not always easy. Certainly, he had his failings and struggled with this challenge as we do. But his writings do offer some advice. In *Christian Behaviour*, he responded to the challenge of continuing to love God and others when you are not sure that you really love them. To this he suggested that we not worry about whether we really love God and those who might be difficult to love. This is not the issue. Instead of getting caught up in the feelings that we believe ought to guide our actions, Lewis suggested that instead we should "Act as *if you did*" have those feelings. Lewis says to focus on God's love for us and to know that God will "give us the *feelings* of love if he pleases."[55] Lewis reminds us that serving God is a matter of the "will" and that if "we are trying to do His will" then we are loving God by serving the needs of others.[56]

Personal Ponderings

Mother Teresa might very well be the best contemporary example that we have of what it means to truly place the needs of others above our own. She took the call of service to the highest level as she obeyed God's call to leave the convent and to serve the poor as she lived among them. Living among them, she realized that many were not only seeking physical needs but also in need of love, respect, and dignity. Thus, she reminded us of Jesus's Parable on the Mount where he taught the beatitudes and called us to serve him by serving others. But in her reading of the parable and in her living out of it, Mother Teresa taught us that people are not only hungry for food but also for love and that people need not just clothing but also dignity.[57]

To respond to Jesus's calling, in 1949 Mother Teresa founded a school in Calcutta where she taught the children of the poorest of the poor. She also learned how to administer basic medical treatment and treated the poor in their own homes.[58]

To serve those who hospitals would not even treat, Mother Teresa rescued the sick and dying from the gutters of the streets. She learned the basics of medical treatment and rented a room in Calcutta to treat and serve the needs of the people who had been abandoned by others. She was helped in her efforts by her pupils, and in 1950 the group became known as the The Missionaries of Charity. Her work eventually spread around the world, as more homes for the dying were established. In 1971, the first home was opened in New York. She also led the early efforts that established homes for those dying from AIDS. She was ultimately recognized with the Nobel Peace Prize and the Pope John XXIII Peace Prize. She refused any awards banquets and insisted that the money be given to the poor, instead, because she believed that earthly rewards only had value if they helped the poor and needy.[59]

Contrary to what society teaches us, Mother Teresa called us to remember that "At the end of our lives, we will not be judged by how many diplomas we have received, how much money we have made or how many great things we have done. We will be judged by 'I was hungry and you gave me to eat. I was naked and you clothed me. I was homeless and you took me in."[60]

Finding Purpose

Why is it so challenging to place the needs of others before our own?

Who has God entrusted you to lead? How do you listen to their needs?

How could you better listen and show empathy to those God has entrusted you to lead?

How can might we learn from the examples of C.S. Lewis and Mother Teresa? Which of their examples or words spoke the loudest to you and your own struggles with serving others? Why?

How will you try to incorporate this lesson into your daily struggles with serving others before yourself?

Finding Scripture

While we have reflected on the Sermon on the Mount before, Mother Teresa's reading of the Scripture invites us to enter Jesus's calling more deeply than most of us may have considered. Her reading of the Scripture reminds us that we can hunger for more than food and desire more than physical clothing and shelter. She also reminds us that Jesus is clear about telling us that we will be judged by how well we live out the Beatitudes. I believe that Mother Teresa is correct; we can't limit ourselves to only reading the Beatitudes on a literal level. We must also go deeper and see the various ways in which people hunger and desire to be sheltered and clothed. We must learn to see and listen with more than our eyes and ears—we must learn to see and hear with our hearts. And our hearts must desire to place the needs or others above our own.

Suggested Scripture Reading and Reflections

Jesus teaches us how we are to serve others in many places. Two of the most direct lessons are in Matthew 5: 1-12 and Matthew 26: 31-46. After reading these Scripture passages, use the following questions to reflect on how well you are serving others.

What besides food could people hunger for? Who do you know who might be hungering or thirsting in this way? How are you helping to meet these needs?

What types of shelter might people need besides housing? How might you help others secure this type of shelter? What can you do?

When have you gotten to know Jesus better by serving others? How might you get to know and serve him better?

Section Three: Courage

The battle is between faith and reason on one side and emotion and imagination on the other.[1]

Going it Alone

Reflections on Lewis's Voyage

On the Island of the Voices, Lucy encounters a task that requires her to leave the others and enter the unknown all alone. And the unknown is a place that has been feared by the inhabitants of the island for many years. They will not enter it because they are afraid—and thus they remain invisible. And the irony, the chief voice tells them "we have been waiting forever so long for a nice little girl"[2] to go upstairs in the magician's house to retrieve the book of spells and utter the spell that will make them visible again.

Why is this ironic? Society has traditionally portrayed and viewed the female and children as the weak and in need of protection. Here, Lewis shows us through Lucy that anyone can be brave and strong. Gender and age does not determine our usefulness.

There are two other important points here that I believe Lewis calls our attention to that are worth noting. One is Lewis's focus on the unknown and finding the courage to embrace it and enter it—alone. The second is fear. He metaphorically plays with fear by making those who are not brave invisible.

Entering the Unknown

Like Lucy, we also find ourselves faced with this task at times. We must venture into unknown territory. This scares us because we do not know what we will face. There is no way to prepare for what we have not previously experienced and thus we often become afraid as we conjure up all of the frightening situations that we might encounter. And sometimes, these images that we create in our imaginations impede us as we refuse to enter places we have not been. Could this be what made the inhabitants of the island invisible? Is this what Lewis wants us to reflect on with his metaphor? If we fail to find the courage to enter the unknown do we begin to threaten our own existence? When we stop living and taking risks, do we begin to cease to exist as we become stagnant? And as we listen to the foolishness of the island dwellers we begin to wonder if Lewis might not also be implying that in our inability to face fear and change we might not also become rather foolish and unintelligent.

Of course, Lucy's immediate reaction to entering the house alone is fear. When she thinks of the unknown she asks "would I have to go upstairs at night?" Here she shows a common fear for all of us—the darkness of the night. And again, Lewis creates a metaphor, as the Chief Voice replies "Oh, daylight, daylight, to be sure. Not at night. No one's asking you to do that. Go upstairs in the dark? Ugh."[3]

Daylight is our faith; darkness is the absence of faith. The magician's house could be seen as God's house—and the upstairs as the realm of God. Here, I find Lewis showing me that doing God's work may often seem like the unknown—and it will be frightening. But if I enter in the daylight—I will not be alone. And I will not be blind. My faith will guide my way and allow me to see. Additionally, I see Lucy's search for a spell to help the invisible people as my call to prayer. In finding prayer, I can call on God to help myself and others.

And yet in praying are we not also entering the unknown? Aren't we also called to trust in what we do not know? In prayer, we must have the courage to believe. And in finding that courage we must let go of our emotions and leave the doubts of our imagination behind.

Letting Go of Fear

Lewis helps us to better understand this in Chapter 11 of *Christian Behaviour*. There he tells us that it is not reason that impedes us and causes us to lose our courage and faith. He argues that "faith is based on reason."[4] Rather, what leads us out of the light and into the darkness is "imagination and emotion."[5] To reiterate his words that I chose to premise this section, "The battle is between faith and reason on one side and emotion and imagination on the other."[6] And you may wonder, how do we know which is reason and which is emotion? To discover this, we must take the time to pause and reflect on what we knew to be true before the situation occurred. We must turn to the wisdom of Scripture and our trusted friends; we must listen to what has been etched in our hearts before the beginning of time. Often we find this by consulting with others. While Edmund and the others fear for her safety, they take the time to listen to Reepicheep, "as no one had ever known Reepicheep to be afraid of anything."[7]

And in deciphering between fear and reason, Reepicheep sorted out what should be done by examining the nature of the act that Lucy intends to perform. And in finding Lucy's reasons "noble and heroic,"[8] he agrees that Lucy should indeed follow her heart. And perhaps that might also be a test for our own actions when we take the time to reflect on whether we should enter the unknown. First, ask ourselves if we are acting in the "daylight"—are we walking in the light of our faith as we enter the unknown. Second, are we acting heroically and with nobility? Will our actions positively affect others? If so, we may courageously enter with the hope to win the battle.

Personal Ponderings

What Lewis shows Lucy doing here is not easy. It is difficult to put aside our emotions and think through what is right and just for us to do—especially when we are facing the unknown. Fear can easily cloud our judgment and convince us that it is reasonable to protect ourselves and to remain in safety. But as Lewis also says in *Christian Behaviour*, these are the times when we must rely on our faith. And he defines this faith as "the art of holding on to things your reason as once accepted, in spite of your changing moods." [9]

This seems simple enough, but in our culture of situational ethics and relativism, we find ourselves bombarded with the notion that our moods should determine our actions. These trends attempt to convince us that there is no right way to act. We should allow our situation to guide our actions, and that even then, the right way to act may depend on the individual.

The time management expert Stephen Covey recounts an instance where he faced this type of thinking at a speaking engagement on a college campus. While speaking at a fraternity-sorority event about the new morality, he encountered several students who rigorously argued that there "are no absolute truths and standards"[10] but rather that "each situation must be looked at in terms of the people involved as well as other factors present."[11] These students were continuing to gain much support for their position as Covey continued to maintain there are "a set of principles that operate independent of any individual"[12]—such as "integrity, moderation, self-discipline, fidelity, and responsibility."[13] Finally, when he realized that he was not getting anywhere, he said: "'Each of us knows in our heart the truth of the matter. We all have a conscience. We all know. And if you will take a few moments and just reflect and listen carefully to what your heart tells you, you will know the answer."[14] While Covey admits that many "sneered and jeered"[15] at this idea, they eventually complied. They closed their eyes and listened to their hearts. And after listening to their hearts for a "full minute of silence,"[16] one of the students who had been arguing the most vigorously in defense of their situational ethics said: "What I heard is not what I have been saying."[17] And another admitted: "I don't know—I just don't know. I'm not certain anymore."[18]

In Covey's example, I believe that these students experienced what Lewis depicts with Lucy and her friends. They found themselves moved by their hearts—by a reason that is not determined by our moods or circumstances. Covey calls this inner voice "True North" and finds that when we take the time to listen to it "we connect with the wisdom of the ages and the wisdom of the heart" and we also "become less a function of the social mirror and more a person of character and conscience."[19]

It is this inner compass that also gives us strength and courage in even the toughest and most frightening times. For example, Viktor E. Frankl, in his book *Man's Search for Meaning*, tells of the daily horrors and anguish he and his fellow inmates faced daily during the Holocaust in a concentration camp. In finding the courage to continue to exist, Frankl said that he and his inmates had to "stop asking about the meaning of life,"[20] which might stir up emotions of fear and self-pity. Instead, they had to reflect on their own "right action" and "right conduct."[21] They needed to look deep within and listen to their hearts to find what was right and just. This allowed them to direct their own thinking when those around them were void of all moral conduct. And in achieving this higher level of thought, Frankl found that humans find the courage "to acknowledge the fact that even in suffering he is unique and alone in the universe. No one can relieve him of his suffering or suffer in his place. His unique opportunity lies in the way in which he bears his burden."[22] That seems to be our true test of courage—how we bear our burdens. Will we turn away or will we go bravely into the light listening to our inner hearts?

Finding Purpose

When have you been afraid to face the unknown? What was the unknown? What did you do?

When have you listened to your inner compass to find good reason and judgment? What did it tell you?

When do you find it most difficult to act courageously? Why?

How could you be more conscious of taking the time to reflect before acting?

What burden are you being asked to carry at this point in your life? How are you bearing it?

Finding Scripture

The Book of Wisdom[1] gives us a chance to reflect on this inner voice that often guides us. The author of this book personifies the gift God gives to us discern from right and wrong. In Wisdom 7, we hear of how Solomon prayed and pleaded for Wisdom to come to him. He also describes her in great detail so that we come to recognize her in our own lives. Wisdom 9 tells us of how Solomon came to recognize Wisdom as a gift from God. He then goes on to share his own prayer for Wisdom with us. In all of these readings, we find a chance to reflect on the presence of Wisdom in our own lives so that we also might use reason to guide us and give us courage when our emotions cloud our judgment. Wisdom 10 especially reassures us that when Wisdom guides us we need not fear, as it recounts the

---

[1] This book is regarded as part of the Bible by Catholics but not by Protestants.

many instances where God's faithful followers were kept from harm and evil.

Suggested Scripture Reading and Reflections

Read through the first ten chapters of Wisdom and reflect on your own encounters with Wisdom. Find strength in courage in the times that God's Wisdom led you and guided you in times of turmoil, fear, and in the unknown. Use the following questions to guide your reflection or to share your thoughts with others.

How would you describe Wisdom? How are your descriptions similar or different from Solomon's?

How do you recognize the presence of Wisdom in your life?

When have you made a decision without wisdom? What was the result? How did you cope with the outcome?

How will you work to nurture Wisdom further in your life?

Why is Wisdom necessary for courage?

Can you have courage without it? Why or why not?

THE VOICE OF INTERVENTION

REFLECTIONS ON LEWIS'S VOYAGE

After Eustace returns to normal, Edmund and Caspian soon find themselves grappling with their own selfishness. The crew soon stumbles upon a deep, blue pool with perfectly clear water. At the bottom, they discover a man that has turned to gold. After experimenting, they discover that the water turns anything that it touches to pure gold. That is when greed rears its angry head. Edmund and Caspian begin to argue over who should be rightful king of the island—as they ponder the value and worth of such a pool. They begin to bicker and argue despite their friendship. Realizing where the battle might lead, Lucy intervenes. She says "Oh, stop it both of you."[22] And then immediately, she gasped and led the others to see what she saw—Aslan.

In this scene, Lewis shows us that each of us has the ability to lose sight of what is important. He also shows us that others can serve as Jesus voice—and redirect us back to the right path. Here, Lucy speaks for Aslan when she tells them to stop it. It is her voice that causes them to pause—and see Aslan. Quickly after, Lewis tells us that they all "looked at one another like people waking from sleep."[23] Caspian then wonders what he was talking about. The gold no longer seems important. And Edward openly questions, "Have I been making an ass of myself?"[24] Here, Lewis shows us that if we listen, Jesus will speak to us (often through our friends and family) and redirect us when sin leads us astray. The key is to listen.

In *C. S. Lewis, My Godfather,* Laurence Harwood tells us how Lewis, as his godfather, was that voice of intervention when Harwood failed his preliminary exams at Oxford. Realizing the effect such a failure might have had on his godson, he promptly wrote to him and reminded him that exams do not always accurately measure the academic aptitudes of a person and that many of the great scholars may not have succeeded if they had to face such exams. Additionally, he advised him to pick up and move on. He also warned him of the danger of "seeking consolation in *Resentment*"[25] for Lewis himself had found it to be "a favourite device of the human mind"[26] to convince oneself that "one has been misused"[27] and to "snap and snarl at the 'system.'"[28] He warned that this type of response "makes man always a bore, usually an ass, sometimes a villain."[29] He also advised that instead of choosing to see himself "as no good" or as a "victim" to instead "write the whole thing off and get on."[30] And in helping Harwood to "get on," Harwood tells us that Lewis's letter "brought great consolation and reassurance," as he "took the advice it contained and set off in a new direction."[31] This new direction also involved the generosity of Lewis's funds, as he paid for Harwood to attend the Royal Agricultural College where Harwood underwent training to become a land agent and surveyor, which eventually led to a successful career with National Trust.

Thus, Lewis shows us not only that we must listen to the voice of intervention. He also shows us that we may also serve as the voice of intervention if we allow Jesus to speak and work through us.

Personal Ponderings

Again, while Lewis's advice to us might seem simple, or (as he tells Harwood) might seem like "easy talking," experience proves it to be sometimes very difficult to listen to the voice of others when we are faced with situations that challenge and torment us. In fact, sometimes we may actually feel that the voice of intervention is wrong and doubt its worth and value.

I was reminded of this lesson the other night while watching the movie *The Shawshank Redemption*. If you have seen the movie, you may recall that the main character, Andy, has been imprisoned for the murder of his wife—even though he didn't commit the murder. Yet, while in prison, Andy refuses to buckle despite the many horrors he faces, and in fact brings hope to many of the inmates. In one of these various scenes, Andy shares with his trusted friend and fellow inmate (Red) his dream to one day open a hotel on the beach of Mexico. Red, who has had his parole rejected many times, finds Andy's hope dangerous. Sensing that Red has lost hope and fearing that Red might one day kill himself if he ever does receive parole (like another former friend and inmate), Andy tells Red that hope has kept Andy alive. He then challenges Red to either "Get busy living or get busy dying." He then makes Red promise that if he ever does get out of prison that he will look for a metal box beneath a stone in a pasture they are both familiar with. Red promises, though it is clear that he fears Andy's notion of hope. Like us, Red questions the voice of intervention that might lead him out of his own misery—even though the voice is a trusted friend.

But, Andy's words "Get busy living or get busy dying," later echo in Red's heart and mind years later when Red does receive parole. When he is tempted to give into fear and despair, he hears the remembered words and promise he made to Andy. Choosing to listen to that voice, he decides to "get busy living" and find the tin box that eventually leads him to his friend Andy. The voice gives him hope and saves his life.

I find the message of this movie to be very similar to Lewis's advice to Harwood. It also resonates of the dangers of letting ourselves "snap and snarl at the system."[32] Rather than becoming bitter about his predicament, Andy found a way to make the best of it and to help others. He found a way out by holding on to hope, and he shared that hope with others by allowing himself to be a voice of intervention for others.

Finding Purpose

When have you found yourself losing sight of reason and giving in to sin? What was the result?

Was there a voice you could have listened to? If so, what did it say? What would have been the result if you had listened?

When have you listened to the voice of a friend or family member and avoided misery? What was his or her advice?

When have you been the voice of intervention for someone else? How did it feel?

How can you become a better listener to discern God's voice in your life?

Finding Scripture

Through the book of Samuel, God directly shows us how he manifests himself to us and through us. When Samuel hears his name called in his sleep, he does not understand who is calling him and believes it to be Eli. This happens three times before Eli realizes that God must be calling Samuel. Eli then explains this to Samuel and advises him to invite God to speak to him and to listen as God's servant. Eli turns out to be correct in his advice to Samuel. But ironically, God's message is not good for Eli. Samuel must tell Eli that God will bring great punishment to Eli's family because Eli did not reprove his sons' blaspheme. While Samuel does not want to deliver the message, he feared how Eli might react. But at Eli's urging, he gives voice to God's message. Eli then knows Samuel's words to be God's and also finds God's punishment just.

We can take many lessons from this Scripture reading. First, we learn how to listen and recognize God's voice in our lives. We also find that sometimes we might need others to help us recognize God's voice and how to respond to God's calling. Second, we see how to be a voice for God to others when Samuel finds courage to deliver an unfavorable message to his friend. It is not always easy to deliver God's messages. Like Samuel, we need to find courage to be the voice of intervention. And, like Eli, we may also find ourselves receiving unwelcome messages from God through the voices of others who are close to us. When we do, we also need to find the courage to accept the truth of the messages and to find God's will to be just.

Suggested Scripture Reading and Reflections

Read through 1 Samuel 3: 1-18. As you read, reflect on how God speaks to Samuel, how Samuel learns to recognize God's voice and how to respond to God, as well as how Samuel finds courage to be God's voice. Additionally, reflect on Eli's role. How does he also serve as God's voice and a receiver of God's voice? Then use the following questions to apply the reading to your own life. You may also want to use the questions to share your experiences with others.

What lessons do you take from Samuel? From Eli? How can you apply these lessons to your daily living?

How does God speak to you? How do you know when it is him? How do you respond?

What role is most difficult for you? To be the voice of God or to be the receiver of God's message? Why? How can you improve in this role?

Letting Go of Ourselves

Reflections on Lewis's Voyage

In *Christian Behaviour,* Lewis tells us that the cardinal virtue of fortitude "includes both kinds of courage—the kind that faces danger as well as the kind that 'sticks it' under pain."[33] After Eustace sheds his scales and rejoins the crew of *The Dawn Treader,* we are told that "he began to be a different boy."[34] But what does this mean? I believe it means that he began to be less prideful. He learned to let go of himself and think of others. While this may seem simple, I believe that Lewis shows it to require a great deal of courage.

For example, once Eustace "began trying to behave well," we also see him engage in "the first brave thing he had ever done."[35] When the crew faces a sea serpent, Eustace forgets about his own safety and needs. Instead, as soon as the sea serpent nears, he courageously "jumped onto the bulwark and began hacking it with all of his might."[36] It does not matter that he fails to kill the serpent. The importance is that he lets go of himself and his fears and bravely tries to help the others.

The scene becomes symbolic for a number of reasons. I believe that the sea serpent could easily be seen metaphorically as Satan—who is often described in scripture as a serpent. Additionally, Satan is often equated with pride—as it led to his fall from God. As Lewis aptly explains, "it was through Pride that the devil became the devil: Pride leads to every other vice: it is the complete anti-God state of mind."[37] And, as Pride leads us to become completely self-absorbed, to combat pride, we must learn to forget ourselves. We need to find the courage to begin thinking of others.

As Eustace begins to think of others and to behave, he also becomes brave and finds the courage to take on the sea serpent, which

I believe symbolically shows him finding the courage to recognize the serpent as evil (the devil) and to "hack at it with all of his might."[38] He begins to fight pride. How can we know for sure? Lewis tells us that "the real test" is that "you forget about yourself altogether."[39] Clearly, Eustace forgets about himself as he jumps toward the serpent and begins to "hack away at it."

Personal Ponderings

Pride has a way of entering all of our lives. Today, I even found it entering my prayer. Worried about a situation that seems out of control, I found myself praying for those whom I felt were to blame. And then I stopped myself ... wasn't I in these thoughts thinking myself above those I was blaming. Could I not also be at fault? Of course, I could. I then found my thoughts interrupted by e-mail letting me know that a new message had arrived.

Another one of those chain emails. Irritated and annoyed that the sender passed it on to me, I glanced at the subject heading. While my next step is usually to delete these messages, this time I hesitated. On the right side, I saw a fabricated email. Beside To: it read "You. Beside From: read "God." The date was "Today" and the subject was "Life." Corny as it might seem, the message in the body of the email was exactly what I needed to hear at the moment. It read:

> This is God. Today I will be handling All of your problems for you. I do Not need your help. So, have a nice day. I love you. P.S. And, remember...If life happens to deliver a situation to you that you cannot handle, do Not attempt to resolve it yourself! Kindly put it in the SFGTD (something for God to do) box. I will get to it in MY TIME. All situations will be resolved, but in My time, not yours.

After reading it, I felt embarrassed and humbled. In my prayer, I had not only been assigning blame to others, but I had been telling God when and how to handle it. I also had blindly believed that by asking God for help I was being humble. But my prayer was not humble at all. In fact, my consumption with fear and anxiety over the situation showed pride and an absence of courage.

To fight my serpent, I needed to do exactly what the email message advised. I needed to turn the situation over to God—to place it in his box and know that God would take care of it his way and in his own time. I needed to give all control to God.

Ironically, the email that had distracted me and irritated me in the midst of my prayer turned out to deliver the message that I needed at the time. As it turns out, God speaks to us even in our distractions. Silently, I said a prayer of thank you to the sender, prayed for forgiveness for the judgment I had made of the person, and humbly I forwarded the message on to others who I also felt might enjoy the message—realizing that they might also become annoyed and frustrated with me, but also praying that God would speak to them as he had to me.

Finding Purpose

When have you battled pride? What was the result?

What shape does your serpent most often take?

How can you find the courage to hack away at it?

What steps can take to let go of yourself? Why is this such a difficult battle for us?

Finding Scripture

In Exodus, we read of the Israelites' constant testing of God, and Moses's repeated examples of serving as God's messenger and vessel. Not only do these examples show Moses as having tremendous courage, they also show his selflessness as he lets go of himself, surrenders to God, and serves the Israelites regardless of the Israelites doubts, verbal abuses, and ungrateful attitudes toward him. One such example shows the physical pain and fatigue that Moses endured in allowing God to work through him. Not long after Moses tapped on a rock with his staff allowing water to pour out of the rock and end the Israelites' thirst, they found war waged upon them byAmalek.

In order to defeat Amalek, Moses finds that he must stand on a hill and hold up the staff of God in his hand. When his arms become tired and he lowers them, Amalek begins to gain advantage in the battle. To help Moses, Aaron and Hur give him a rock to sit upon, and they hold his arms up for him.

Here we find that letting go of pride not only requires us to allow God to work through us, but sometimes, we may find that we must admit our own weakness and allow others to help us. Eustace also found this to be the case. When his attempts to cut the serpent away failed, he had to rely on Reepicheep's wisdom to remove the serpent's tail from the ship. In both instances, we find that letting go of ourselves may sometimes require us to humbly welcome the help of others.

Suggested Scripture Reading and Reflections

Read through Exodus 17: 8-13, then use the following questions to reflect on your own battles with pride.

When have you found yourself tired and fatigued in doing God's work? How did God offer you help? What was your response?

Why is it difficult to accept help from others? Why is it necessary?

In what situations might God be sending you help for his work? How are you responding?

Facing Darkness

Reflections on Lewis's Voyage

After the crew of the *Dawn Treader* successfully helped the Dufflepuds find happiness again, the magician mended the stern of their ship and the crew returned to the sea where they sailed onward in their adventure. Yet, on the thirteenth day of this adventure, they begin to encounter a darkness that Lewis tells us to imagine as "looking into the mouth of a railway tunnel."[40] While we may be able to see the initial twists and turns at the beginning of tunnel, there is a point where all light disappears "without a sharp dividing line"[41] and the track seems to "vanish altogether into smooth and solid blackness."[42] This is the type of darkness the crew faced. And as they approached, they became fearful for they did not know what lurked in the darkness or what they would face. As the king and leader, Caspian asks "Do we go into this?"[43] The captain advises against it, as do the sailors and Edmund. Lucy and Eustace, the crew members with the most recent lessons in bravery, remain silent but secretly "feel glad inside"[44] that the consensus of the crew seems to be to turn around and avoid the darkness. And it seems that they will turn around until "the clear voice" of Reepicheep "broke into the silence."[45] In answer to Caspian's question "Do we go into this?," Reepicheep responds "And why not? Will someone explain to me why not?"[46] He then continues to wonder if the notion of turning around might not have "proceeded from cowardice."[47] He then goes on to say "I hope it will never be told in Narnia that a company of noble and royal persons in the flower of their age turned tail because they were afraid of the dark."[48]

Drinian, the captain, then voices the reasonable question that we might also ask "But what manner of use would it be ploughing through that blackness?"[49] Reepicheep quickly responds to what seems a logical question and may be one of the toughest lessons of our own faith and Christian courage:

> Use, Captain? If by use you mean filling our bellies or our purses, I confess it will be no use at all. So far as I know we did not set sail to look for things useful but to seek honour and adventure. And here is as great adventure as ever I heard of, and here, if we turn back no little impeachment of our honours.[50]

Not surprisingly, Reepicheep's words were not welcomed. Recognizing the truth and wisdom of his words, they knew they would not be able to turn around. Caspian shows his struggles with it as he says "Oh, bother you, Reepicheep. I almost wish we'd left you at home."[51] I have to admit I might have said the same and can remember times of frustration when I said almost the same when someone tried to turn my thinking around and make me face what I would rather not. But not being able to deny the truth of Reepicheep's argument, he admits "I suppose we shall have to go on."[52] However, not too different from us, he makes one last ditch effort by calling on another respected member of the crew who is also known for bravery and wisdom. Knowing that Lucy had just earned much respect in saving the Dufflepuds, he hopes that she might counter Reepicheep. We can almost hear the pleading and hope in his voice as he says "Unless Lucy would rather not?"[53]

Lucy, feeling like Caspian, that "she would very much rather not,"[54] bravely disregards her fears and feelings and instead says "I'm game."[55] And Drinian asks if Caspian would "at least order lights."[56] Agreeing that lights were a reasonable and good request, Caspian responds "by all means."[57] And so the ship, "with three lanterns, at the stern, the prow, and the masthead, were all lit"[58] proceeding into the darkness, while the crew looked behind them "in the sunshine."[59]

In this scene, Lewis teaches us much about our Christian tendencies and responsibilities. As discussed in previous sections, the voyage of the crew and ship really signifies our own Christian voyage. And like the crew encounters hardships and challenges to overcome, so do we as we sail into the adventures into our own Christian faith. But the darkness that they encounter in this scene, I believe brings us face to face with one of the toughest of all Christian challenges—to continue to venture forth into unknown and frightening realms when we do not know where they will take us. To go boldly where no man has gone before . . . Thus, it is fitting to wonder if Lucy might respond to Caspian's last ditch desperation for her to call off the journey. If you remember from the scene in "Going it Alone," Lucy had just faced a similar situation. She had to enter the magician's house all by herself, not knowing what she would face. Calling on the bravery that she had found within herself, she let go of her fears and said "I'm game," knowing that this time her challenge would be in dark.

To further elaborate on what Lewis teaches me here, I turn to his thoughts on Christian Faith as discussed in *Christian Behaviour*. As I mentioned previously (Going it Alone), Lewis tells us that faith is "holding on to things your reason has once accepted, despite your changing moods."[60] And Lucy is faithful in realizing that she must be brave despite her fears, that she must ignore her feelings and mood, in deciding that she must listen to and agree with Reepicheep. Lewis admits that he had these moods that made his ability to meet the challenges of his Christian faith "unlikely."[61] But like Lucy, he learned why "Faith is such a necessary virtue."[62] As he aptly explains, Faith allows us to tell our "moods 'where to get off'"[63] so that we don't become "a creature dithering to and fro, with its beliefs really dependent on the weather and the state of its digestion."[64] And here is the irony. Reepicheep, a mouse, a creature most humans would expect to "dither to and fro" with his emotions and decisions based on weather or cheese, reminds the crew and us of the responsibility and mission.

As Christians we are not called to be cowards. We are called to bravery and nobility. We are not to "turn tail" because we are afraid of the "dark." Nor are we to turn to reason and logic, as Drinian echoes our question "What is the use?" Reason misleads us in these situations because faith is not always reasonable. As Reepicheep reminds us, we do not measure the success or call of our Christian duties and responsibilities with the measures of this material world, such as "purse" (money) or our "bellies" (food and survival). Clearly, Lewis reminds us here that Christ entered the world and left it poor and dependent on others for food and shelter. Like Caspian and the crew, we may find ourselves at a loss of argument with Reepicheep in this scene. And, as we find ourselves turning for support in a last ditch effort, we might listen to Lewis echoing Lucy's voice "I'm game," as we recall that he turned away from atheism and embraced Christianity. We can also wisely choose to guide our ship with the light of our three lanterns, the Father, the Son, and the Holy Spirit.

If you find it hard to turn away from the reasons of the world and meet the challenges of Christianity—not knowing where it will lead you, you are not alone. But Lewis does offer us some advice on how to avoid "being reasoned out of it"[65] and to avoid "drift[ing] away,"[66] as the ship and crew of the *Dawn Treader* came close to doing. To avoid drifting on our own voyages, he found that one "must train the habit of faith."[67] And to do this, he advises:

- Recognizing that you "*have* moods."[68]
- Spending time with the "doctrines" of Christianity daily through prayer, reading and attending church—to keep our faith "fed."[69]
- Humbly admitting that "every power of thinking or of moving your limbs from moment to moment is given you by him."[70]

Personal Ponderings

As I reflect on this scene from *The Voyage of the Dawn Treader* and Lewis's advice for us for growing in the practice of our faith, I find many parallel themes in the life of St. Elizabeth Ann Seton. In fact, I am sure that she also must have seen a similar island of darkness approaching her as she and her husband embarked on a sea voyage to Italy. She and her husband had already been challenged with many hardships in the past five years. After her father-in-law passed away (four short years after they married), they found themselves raising her husband's seven siblings and three young children of their own. Soon after, they faced the bankruptcy of their business. Now with five children and limited funds, her husband Will was ill with tuberculosis. A trip to the warm climate of Italy was their last hope for a cure.

For Elizabeth the darkness represented what would become of her husband, her children, her family, and her finances. As she left with her husband and eldest child, she relied on God to calm her fears and lead her through the darkness that loomed ahead. Later she found that the darkness included the death of her husband, her sister-in-law, two daughters, and great poverty. How did she cope? How did she avoid drifting away? A biography of her from the Emmetsburg Historical Society says "She faced each day with eyes of faith, looking forward to eternity."[71] It also notes that she did this by devoting her life to God's divine will, sacred Scripture, and the Eucharist.

As she sailed through her darkness of adversity, keeping her eyes on faith gave her a charming disposition that led others to want to be around her. It also helped her to educate, raise her children and educate them and others in their Christian faith, as she worked in orphanages, served the poor, and founded the Sisters of Charity Order.

The journey of her faith also called her to examine her Episcopalian faith and heritage, as she considered becoming Catholic. This put her under a great deal of stress and scrutiny because her family and community did not approve of her converting to her Catholicism. In fact, her decision to became Catholic caused her even greater economic distress as she lost teaching positions when Protestant community members refused to let her educate their children. But to reiterate what Reepicheep told his crew members and what Elizabeth likely told her family members, we do not begin our Christian journey in pursuit of money or earthly food. Elizabeth sought the Catholic Church for a different kind of food—a spiritual food. She converted to Catholicism so that she could share in the Eucharist. She hungered for the Body of Christ, even when her family and friends questioned her reasoning and likely wondered "What's the use?"

But because Elizabeth had "fed" her faith daily with prayer and Scripture, she did not listen to their questions or disapproval. Instead, she continued into the darkness following God's divine will for her life. I am sure this was not always easy. Certainly, she had to have feared for her children and her very life at times. Likely, she shed tears and had moments of frustration. But her biography and writings reveal that she found her courage in her faith.

Finding Purpose

When have you faced an island of darkness? How did you feel? What did you do?

How did you find faith?

When has reason threatened your faith? Did you drift away? If so, who or what brought you back?

How could you do a better job of facing each day "with the eyes of faith"?

How do you live God's divine will? How do you find courage to deal with the challenges?

Finding Scripture

St. Elizabeth Ann Seton spent much time reading and reflecting on Scripture. In times of adversity, it gave her comfort, courage and hope. One of her favorite passages was Psalm 23,[72] which personifies how she lived her life. Realizing that the Lord was her shepherd, she followed him and obeyed his will. In green pastures, she found rest, and when walking through the valleys of darkness, she did not fear evil or harm. She knew that by following in God's footsteps only goodness and mercy would follow her.

Spend some time reading Psalm 23. Then, use the following questions to reflect on the meaning of the psalm in your life.

Suggested Scripture Reading and Reflections

When are you most likely to see God as your shepherd? How does he take care of your needs? Do you want? Should you?

Where is he currently leading you? Are you following? What causes you to pause? Why?

What valley of darkness are you currently walking through? What fears do you need to let go of that are in your valley of darkness? How will you find the courage?

What green pastures of rest has God given you? Are you resting?

How can you be more mindful and trusting that only goodness and mercy will follow you?

In what situations might God be sending you help for his work? How are you responding?

Finding Prayer

Reflections on Lewis's Voyage
Good and Evil

In chapter one of *God in the Dock*, Lewis responds to an article by C.E.M Joad that presented good and evil as two dual forces operating in the world. Lewis's response to this dualist perception of good and evil causes us to reflect on our own perceptions of good and evil. For, as Lewis aptly explains, if we see God and Satan (good and evil) as opposing forces then we are seeing them as two viable and equal forces to choose from. The "moral difficulty" with this dualistic notion of good and evil "is that Dualism gives evil a positive, substantive, self-consistent nature, like that of good."[73] And then our "allegiance"[74] to one becomes merely a preference to one over the other. Lewis argues that "a sound theory of value demands something different. It demands that good should be original and evil a mere perversion; that good should be the tree and evil the ivy ... the good should be able to exist on its own while evil requires the good on which it is parasitic."[75] In this understanding of good and evil, we see that evil cannot exist without good—thus they are not of equal spheres. To further explain this concept, Lewis goes on to clarify that Christian recognizes "that if the Michael is really in the right and Satan really in the wrong this must mean that they stand in two different relations to somebody or something far further back, to the ultimate ground of reality itself."[76]

And I believe this distinction makes all the difference in how we approach situations that may cause us fear and anxiety. If we perceive God as good—"the ultimate ground of reality"[77]—we can then confidently turn to that source when facing darkness and evil because we know that good is stronger, right, and in control of the evil and darkness. Lewis shows us this with the character of Lucy, as the *Dawn Treader* faces the Dark Island.

Feeling the darkness and evil of the island, Lucy (not unlike us) becomes frightened as the darkness surrounds them and the crew gives way to anxiety and they imagine even the rowers of the boat to be moaning "we shall never get out, never get out." And then in addition to these gloomy thoughts, the stranger who they pulled from the dark water suddenly "sat up and burst out into a horrible screaming laugh," leading us to wonder if he might not be possessed by the dark force. He then gives loud voice to all of their internal fears—"Never get out! That's it of course. We shall never get out. What a fool I was to have thought they would let me go so easily as that." Can you imagine how you might have felt if you were on the ship? Surely, it conjures up images of the haunted ship in Coleridge's "Rime of the Ancient Mariner" where the entire crew died and became taken over by evil spirits. Or perhaps the recent movie *Pirates of the Caribbean?* Surely, Lucy had reason to fear. And Lewis calls us to reflect on times where we also feared evil.

But, he also uses this scene to help us reflect on the Christian perception of good and evil. He shows us that good and light is more powerful. He reminds us that Christ defeated sin and evil. Thus, by recognizing this and turning to God in prayer, we also defeat the blackness of evil.

Lewis shows us this when in the midst of the stranger's screaming she "leant her head on the edge of the fighting top and whispered, 'Aslan, Aslan, if ever you loved us at all, send us help now.'"[78] Lucy turns to prayer. She turns to good, to Aslan. And in doing so, she recognizes that the force of good is stronger and more powerful. And in recognizing this through prayer, Lewis shows us that she began to feel hope. While "the darkness did not grow any less ... she began to feel a little—a very, very little—better."[79] I appreciate Lewis's realism here—for he tells us that even in turning to prayer, the darkness did not immediately disappear. And he does not sensationalize it by telling us she felt all better. He tells us she felt a little better. This is important. Sometimes when we find the confidence to pray, we become discouraged that the situation does not immediately get better after we pray. Here, we find that in prayer we will mentally find some relief and courage—to continue the journey and battle against evil. But the battle may not end immediately.

Stages of Hope

He also shows us that the crew found hope in stages as they found their way out of the grasp of evil and darkness—but the key was Lucy's prayer. After her prayer and her bit of mental relief, one of the crew members sees a "tiny speck of light ahead."[80] While this did not "alter the surrounding darkness,"[81] Lewis tells us that "whole ship was lit up as if by a searchlight."[82] And in looking "along the beam," Lucy saw a cross and eventually an albatross (again I find parallels to Coleridge's "Rime of the Ancient Mariner"). The Albatross then circled three times (perhaps signaling the Trinity?) and then "perched for an instant on the crest of the gilded dragon at the prow. It called out in a strong sweet voice what seemed to be words."[83] And while no one else understood those words, Lewis tells us that Lucy "knew that as it circled the mast it had whispered to her, 'Courage, dear heart,' and the voice, she felt sure was Aslan's, and with the voice of a delicious smell breathed in her face."[84] And almost immediately after seeing the bird, "in a few moments the darkness turned into a greyness ahead, and then, almost before they dared to begin hoping, they had shot out into the sunlight.... And all at once everybody realized that there was nothing to be afraid of and never had been."[85]

Lewis gives us much to ponder in this scene. In addition to showing that good is stronger and more powerful than evil. He also gives us repeated images of light and connects it with hope. After calling for help in prayer, Lucy and the others are able to look beyond the darkness and see the rays of light—no matter how tiny and far off it might be. Additionally, he shows us that in the ability to pray and hope, we will also be able to recognize signs such as the cross and the albatross that will lead us, guide us and give us courage. The cross symbolically represents the victory of Christ's crucifixion—where evil was defeated and we were saved from the clutches of evil, sin, and death. The albatross (a symbol of sin to Coleridge's Mariner) becomes the voice of the Holy Spirit telling us to have courage and know that the darkness will not harm us. The sunlight reminds us that one day we will completely emerge from the darkness and walk only in the light of God—and then we (like the crew) will find that there really was nothing to fear at all.

Here, Lewis reminds us that we must not see ourselves caught in between a battle of equal and opposing forces, as such a dualistic outlook of good and evil might lead us to despair, depression, darkness, and doom. Rather, recognizing that evil is but a perversion of good—a force that cannot even exist without the ultimate source of goodness—allows us to cling to only that which is good, confidently knowing that good will always win. This outlook strips evil and darkness of its power. It allows us to find hope in prayer and to keep our eyes on the symbols of faith. There we are reminded that Jesus already won our battle against evil for us. And so, we have nothing to fear.

Personal Ponderings

What amazes me as I write this section on good, evil, and prayer, is how it ties in so directly to the Scripture readings I was called to ponder this Sunday and with our pastor's homily. When I organized the outline for this book and reflected on the scene with Lucy discussed above, I had considered the importance of prayer and Lewis's desire for us to reflect on perception of good and evil—but I had not yet had the experience of this Sunday's Mass. And looking back at Lewis's writing and its relation to this scene in *The Dawn Treader* has caused me to pause yet again and reflect on the presence of evil in this world and our relation to it. And not surprisingly, I find Lewis to be very insightful in his advice on how to perceive our relationship to good and evil.

This past Sunday, the Gospel reading (Mark 1:21-28) tells of a man possessed by an unclean spirit who directly calls out and acknowledges Jesus as the Holy One sent by God and then questions Jesus on what he plans to do with him and the other evil, unclean spirits. Jesus calmly casts the unclean spirit out of the man and goes about his teaching. Not surprisingly, the crowd gathered to listen to Jesus was amazed, and the story of Jesus driving out the evil spirit spread rather quickly.

At first reading, this passage becomes somewhat unsettling because it draws our attention to the reality that evil spirits do exist and are at work in our world. And we might be tempted to fear this acknowledgment—if, and only if, we don't return to the realization that Jesus has already conquered evil. It has no power or control over us unless we allow it to. One of the ways we might allow it to have control over us is to see it as an opposing and equal force of good—which it is not. Jesus clearly shows us this as he calmly and effortlessly dispels it and orders it out of the man in the synagogue. And this was before his crucifixion that freed us from the confines of sin and death.

As our pastor explained, we do acknowledge evil, and when necessary, practice the rite of exorcism—as Christ also did. But, the key is realizing that evil cannot have power or control over us unless we allow it to have that power. One tool of evil is fear. And how do we overcome fear—by turning to God in prayer. Perhaps the best example of this is the Lord's Prayer—which Jesus taught us to pray. In the prayer, Jesus teaches us to ask that we are not allowed into temptation and that God deliver us from evil (Matthew 6:9-14).

Finding Purpose

In the past, how have you viewed the forces of good and evil? How might remembering that the forces are not equal forces give you hope in times of turmoil?

When have you felt or encountered the presence of evil? How did you respond? What was the result?

How do you pray? How does it help you to find hope?

When has prayer opened your eyes to the signs of your faith and kept you focused on good rather than evil? What signs gave you hope?

Finding Scripture

Through Lewis's reflections on good and evil and his scene in *The Dawn Treader* (discussed above), we are reminded of the images of lightness and darkness for good and evil. Throughout Scripture light represents good and darkness represents evil. Light conjures up warmth, life, happiness, and the ability to see, while darkness reminds us of the cold, death, despair, and a lack of seeing. Thus, it is no surprise that we would associate good with light and evil with darkness.

Directly following the passage where Jesus teaches us how to pray the Lord's Prayer, he gives us some guidance about how to live so that we avoid evil (Matthew 6:22-23). He tells us that the eye is the lamp of the body, and if our eye sees correctly and is sound, our body will be filled with light. But if our eye is not seeing correctly, our body will be filled with darkness.

Again, we find lightness and darkness representing good and evil. Here it seems that in order to be filled with light we must keep our eyes on God. This reminds me again of the scene we just reflected on in *The Dawn Treader*. When Lucy, turns to Aslan in prayer, she finds hope and soon the entire ship lit up. The ship could be seen as a body. It is lit up because Lucy led the crew to focus on the tiny bean of light ahead. Her prayer led the crew to hope. I think this might be what Jesus is telling us also. When we keep our eyes on him, when we turn to him in prayer, we find hope. And then our body becomes lit up in faith and becomes a beacon of hope for others. Thus, we have the potential to help our faith community light up like the ship—to recognize that we are the Body of Christ. Seeing in his presence in the Eucharist also helps us to see ourselves lit up together as the Body of Christ. Thus, worshipping together in prayer and the Sacrament of the Eucharist fills our body with light—as our eyes become focused on the treasures of heaven rather than this earth.

But if we keep our eyes focused on the treasures of this earth, we will find despair as they decay, are destroyed, or stolen from us. Keeping our eyes on this world will only lead us to darkness—to depression, anxiety, and fear. Losing all sense of hope, our eyes fill our bodies with a negativity of darkness that may also lead others astray.

Suggested Scripture Reading and Reflections

After reading Matthew 6:9-22, use the following questions to guide your reflection about prayer and its relation to good and evil in your life.

What direction do you find about prayer in Jesus's teaching of the Lord's Prayer?

Where is your eye currently directed? How is it affecting your outlook on life? Are you filled with light? Or darkness?

How can you keep your eye focused on the treasures of heaven? When do your eyes become most distracted? Why? How has this affected your faith? The faith of others?

In what sense do our eyes affect the body of our faith community? How can we help others in our community be filled with light and see themselves as part of the Body of Christ?

How can you use prayer more effectively to avoid darkness? How might this lead others out of darkness?

Friends and Enemies

Reflections on Lewis's Voyage

Before Eustace has his transformation, he tells us in his diary that he and Reepicheep do not get along. In fact, we get the sense that they are often at odds when Eustace refers to Reepicheep as "that little spy,"[77] as Reepicheep caught him sneaking a cup of water from the water cask. He also calls him "the dangerous little brute"[78] when he angrily rants about being forced to apologize to Reepicheep.

But after Eustace changes, we get a sense that they became civil to one another and at times acted as friends. We see them playing chess right before the sea serpent takes hold of the ship. Losing twice to Reepicheep in chess causes a bit of Eustace's old disagreeable self to emerge, but we then see both Eustace and Reepicheep bravely take charge in trying to defeat the sea serpent. In fact, we are told that Eustace's attempt to cut away the sea serpent was "the first brave thing he had ever done."[79]

In these two characters, I wonder if Lewis might have been showing us that friends can take on different forms. While some friends are close and always agree, sometimes friends may seem more like our adversaries. They are similar to us but different enough from us that we always seem to be at odds. These types of friends challenge us and bring out the best and worst in us. They test us and require courage to maintain the friendship because they do not always tell us what we want to hear. I imagine this to be the type of friendship that Reepicheep and Eustace shared.

I also wonder if this isn't the type of friendship Lewis shared with Owen Barfield. For in *Surprised by Joy*, he tells us that Arthur and Barfield were two different types of friends. While Arthur was the type of friend with whom he could share all of his "most secret delights."[80] And, Barfield was the type of friend with whom he "disagreed about everything."[81] He describes this type of friendship as "fascinating" and "infuriating" because while you share interests you approach them "all at a different angle."[82] In fact, he says with this type of relationship you are "often more like mutually respectful enemies than friends."[83] But the advantage to such a friendship is that "you modify another's thought; out of this perpetual dogfight a community of mind and deep affection emerge."[84] And as Lewis notes that Barfield "changed me a good deal more than I him,"[85] I wonder if this might not also be the case with Reepicheep's effect on Eustace.

Personal Ponderings

I think all of us can relate to the type of friendship that Lewis depicts here. In fact I can't imagine a family without this type of relationship among its members. I remember always being at odds with my younger brother. My parents could attest that we constantly argued and fought and drove everyone crazy. Yet, he is now one of my closest siblings, and I think we would both agree that in our disagreements we often challenged each other and brought out the best in each other. So that out of our "dogfights" a better person emerged.

I believe this is often the case with parents and children. Do you remember going through adolescence and often arguing with your parents—feeling that they could never understand? At times, didn't you feel that they knew absolutely nothing about you or life? And then later, while you may not still completely agree, you begin to respect them and realize that they knew much more than you gave them credit for. And, you begin to realize that much of their influence has shaped you into who you have become.

As a mother of teenagers, I now get to feel as my parents felt. I now know the frustration of trying to guide, nurture, and love children who fight me almost every step of the way. They argue with me and act as though I know nothing about them. And sometimes, I see and realize that they know more than I give them credit for. Loving and respecting each other in these types of relationships takes a great deal of courage. Sometimes it is very tempting to give up and to cease defending what you know to be true. Other times, you want to end the relationship completely. In those times, we need to find the courage of our faith and continue to love and respect as God loves and respects us. And in the end, we will likely find that the relationship has changed us and shaped us for the better. As Lewis explained, "out of this perpetual dogfight a community of mind and deep affection emerge."[86]

Finding Purpose

What relationships are most important in your life? Why?

How does maintaining these relationships require courage?

Do you have a friend who at times seems more like an enemy—in the sense of friendship Lewis describes? How has this relationship shaped you into a better person?

How do you find courage to remain in relationships that are difficult? How do you find the courage to love and respect those people you often disagree with? To love as God loves?

Finding Scripture

As shown in scene above with Reepicheep and Eustace, relationships within communities can bring strife and discord. Our faith community is no different than the crew of the *Dawn Treader* in that we often find ourselves at strife and tempted to judge others. But James reminds us (James 2:1-8) that we must not discriminate by outward appearances or any other means in forming relationships with each other. We must love and respect one another no matter what their status or appearance. James reminds us that Jesus's commandment is clear—we must love our neighbor as ourselves. Remembering this command may guide us when we find ourselves challenged and frustrated in our relationships.

Suggested Scripture Reading and Reflections

As you reflect on the relationships and friendships in your life that may be causing you strife and discord, read James 2:1-11. Then, use the questions that follow to explore the nature of your relationship and discord.

What prejudices do you bring to your relationships? Why?

When have you judged someone in your life because of his or her outward appearances? How does their appearance affect the way you treat him or her? Do you value their opinions less because of the way they look?

How can you look beyond appearances and love and value others as you do yourself? How can you do a better job of respecting and listening to others?

According to James, what will be the result if we don't look beyond our prejudices?

WORRIED SICK

REFLECTIONS ON LEWIS'S VOYAGE

When Reepicheep jumps over the side of the boat into the dark waters where Lucy, Drinian, and Edmund had just seen sea people, Drinian becomes so frightened and worried about Reepicheep's safety that he was "put in a bad temper."[87] I am sure Lewis often felt this way as he worried about his brother. We get a sense of this in a letter to his brother dated 21 February 1932. At the time, Warren was in Shanghai and danger of an attack from the Japanese. In the letter he writes of his relief in hearing from his brother, but also admits that it "does not bear at all on the source of the anxiety."[88] He then goes on to describe two frightening pictures that his anxiety has conjured in his mind.

Much like Drinian, Lewis finds himself emotionally upset by worry for the safety of a loved one. Toward the end of the letter, he mentions prayer and wonders if it might be useful. As he has not yet completely converted over to Christianity at this point in his life, he does not find the complete relief and solace from prayer that he later finds. But the fact that his mind immediately turns to the notion of prayer when he is in the midst of anxiety is telling. And perhaps this might also remind us of ourselves. When anxious and worried, don't we also realize that we shouldn't be? Deep down don't we, like Lewis, know that our worry will not in any way "alter the course of events"?[89] And don't we also almost naturally turn to some type of prayer—even though we might question its value?

It seems that this leads us back to faith and courage. As Christians, we are called to turn all of our worries over to God—to find the courage, to act with faith, and to know that if we do, God will be the one in us doing the work. And while we may be able to accept this more readily for ourselves, I believe the true test in courage comes in realizing this also to be true for those we love. We must also have the courage to trust that others are also listening to God and allowing him to work in them. This means we must let go of anxiety and allow God to work in them—knowing that God has a plan and that he knows best.

Lewis eventually learns this as well. For in reflecting on the question of how our actions relate to our faith and salvation, Lewis replies that "Faith in Christ is the only thing to save you from despair ... and out of that Faith in Him good actions eventually come."[90] He then supports his finding with Philippians 2:12-13, reminding us that we are to "work out [our] own salvation with fear and trembling"[91] knowing that "it is God who worketh" in us.[92] Thus, Lewis reminds us that our fear and trembling should not be out of worry for our safety or others's safety, but rather that we are doing God's will. And then, we can ease those fears by remembering that God is really the one doing the work—and thus our prayers should be for guidance to know what God wills of us.

In this scene, Reepicheep acts out of natural inclination. He does not fear. And in following that inclination, he discovers that the water is sweet and that he is near the end of the world—where he believes he is destined to travel. Reepicheep lets go of his fears and acts as he believes he is called to act. Drinian, overcome with fear, loses sight of what Reepicheep has been called to do and loses his spiritual focus. Finding himself in a bad temper from anxiety and worry, he reprimands Reepicheep and causes the entire crew to become fearful for Reepicheep. Of course, this was all for naught—as Reepicheep safely returns with the knowledge he needed for continuing his calling.

Through this short scene, Lewis calls our attention to the different ways that Christians act. And, I believe that he finds Reepicheep to be the better role model. Yet, I think Lewis may have seen himself in Drinian—as we might also.

Personal Ponderings

As we listen to Drinian yell "Drat that mouse!"[93] and proclaim that Reepicheep is "more trouble than all of the rest of the ship's company put together,"[94] we may even wonder if Drinian likes Reepicheep. But on closer reading and understanding, we soon recall the times that others may have reacted the same way about our own actions. And while their yelling may have made us feel unliked at the time, we later realized that their reactions came from fear for our safety. Like Reepicheep, they worried that we might not return and that they would have to go on living without us.

Lewis confirms this to be the case when he tells us:

> All this didn't mean that Drinian really disliked Reepicheep. On the contrary he liked him very much and was therefore frightened about him, and being frightened put him in a bad temper—just as your mother is much angrier with you for running out in front of a car than a stranger would be.[95]

Here in this scene, Lewis reminds me of myself in two roles. I find myself as a mother. How often do I needlessly worry about my children's safety and often find myself angrily reprimanding them—when I would be better to give them a hug? Of course, this doesn't mean that I shouldn't teach them and guide them about dangers of this world. But it does remind me that I need to allow them to face dangers that might be part of God's plan.

As I reflect on this difficult calling, to let go and let God work in my children. I am reminded of the times that my parents feared for my safety and became angry about my actions. Sometimes they were correct; my choices were not in my best interest. But other times, their reprimands were out of fear that was unwarranted. Sometimes

I was taking the path that I was called to take. And while it may have involved danger, God knew that it would be ok. And I felt deep down that it would be ok.

How do we know the difference? It is certainly not easy. I have found discernment, scripture and prayer to be helpful. I have also found if I am quiet in my prayer and ask for guidance, I almost always hear an inner voice directing me on how to act. This voice is not always easy to listen to. Often it requires me to act in ways that are very challenging and to face situations that I would rather not face. It requires that I rely on my faith to act with courage.

As our country continues to help Iraq, I am sure our soldiers listen to this voice daily as they find the courage to face danger and death—but in doing so they also take comfort in the knowledge that they are helping others. Certainly, their families must fear for their safety. But when knowing that their loved ones are doing what they are called to do—lay down their lives for others—they find the courage to accept and support their family member's decision to join the military forces in fighting terrorism. This is not easy. It is a daily battle; but as Lewis reminded us, this is how Scripture teaches us to act.

Finding Purpose

When have you acted like Drinian? Why? What was the result?

When have you been in Reepicheep's position? Who became upset with you? Why?

How did you know that your decision to face danger was justified?

Which role do you struggle with most? Reepicheep's? Drinian's? How can you find more courage in that role?

Finding Scripture

The most perfect example of acting in God's will with courage is Jesus. He allowed himself to be crucified and put to death because it was God's will for us to have eternal life. And in Jesus's perfect surrender and obedience to God's will, our sins were forgiven and we were given the gift of eternal life. Surely, Mary feared for her son and knew great sorrow as he acted on God's will. But, she also knew that Jesus was doing God's will and thus found courage in knowing that her son would save us. As she obediently carried out God's will for her to give birth to Jesus, she also allowed Jesus to carry out God's will.

Most of us cannot even fathom finding the courage to face such a death. We struggle with finding courage to carry out our daily challenges. But in looking at Jesus's example, we find his source of courage. In John 17:1-26, we see and hear Jesus's prayer. In his words, we find a model for our own prayer. We also find our work is not of this world or to be measured by the standards of this world but rather of the next world. We are called to let go of our worry and anxiety and bring others to God in Jesus's name. And in Jesus's name we find love, protection, and courage.

Suggested Scripture Reading and Reflections

Read John 17:1-26. Then, use the questions that follow to reflect on how prayer might help you find courage to do God's will and to let go of your worry and anxiety.

When you are anxious and worried, how do you pray?

How might you use Jesus's prayer in this passage as a model for your own prayer?

What anxieties and worries are burdensome for you today?

How does this passage give you comfort and courage?

SECTION FOUR: JUSTICE

Justice means much more than the sort of thing that goes on in law courts.[1]

MAKING LAWS JUST

REFLECTIONS ON LEWIS'S VOYAGE

Lewis presents us with our challenge of justice when Caspian and the others find themselves captured by slave traders. Wanting to investigate the source of such cruelty, Caspian doesn't reveal his identity until he later meets Lord Bern (one of the seven lords he had sought out to find). In hearing Lord Bern's story, Caspian discovers that Governor Gumpas is responsible for the slave trading—which Lord Bern has on countless occasions argued "to crush" and described as "vile traffic in man's flesh." [2]

Upon further investigation, Caspian learns from Lord Bern that Gumpas defends his actions as being done "in the King's name."[3] And when Caspian confronts Gumpas, the governor defends his actions by arguing that the trade has made Narrowhaven "the great centre of the trade"[4] and claims that Caspian is too young and inexperienced to understand the economic gains, as well as the nature of "progress and development."[5] Caspian will hear none of it. He responds:

> Tender as my years may be, I believe I understand the slave trade from within quite well as your sufficiency. And I do not see that it brings into the islands meat or bread or wine or timber or cabbages or books or instruments of music or horses or armour or anything else worth having. But whether it does or not, it must be stopped.[6]

I believe that Lewis crafts this scene so that we will reflect on our own practices that we justify. Like Gumpas, we often use measures and assessments of our actions that do not really look at the nature of the actions from, as Caspian says here, "within." This scene reminds me of Lewis's advice in *Christian Behaviour* where he discusses "the difference between doing some particular just or temperate action and being a just or temperate man."[7] He goes on to explain three reasons for making the distinction: 1) "right actions done for the wrong reason do not help to build the internal quality or character called virtue." 2) God wants more than "obedience to a set of rules.... He really wants *people of a particular sort*. 3) If you do not have the qualities of justice within you, "no external conditions could make [you] happy with the strong, unshakable kind of happiness God intends for us."[8]

Thus, when Gumpas attempts to justify his actions by arguing that the slave trade has brought profit and wealth to the people of Narrowhaven and to Caspian's kingdom, we see the type of thinking and logic that has justified many immoral acts in the past. In fact, we may even hear our own reasoning and thinking through Gumpas. But through Caspian, Lewis allows us to see a "temperate man" who courageously looks beyond the material reasons and profits. Rather, Caspian looks "within" and knows that slavery violates human principles and also sees it as Lord Bern described "vile traffic in man's flesh." As having been captured and treated as a slave himself, he sees it from the eyes of a human rather than through the eyes of profit. And he courageously puts an end to it.

Personal Ponderings

As I reflect on Lewis's challenge to look within to consider our actions and the actions of society, I can't help but think of Harriet Beecher Stowe, who used her literary abilities to bring our country to look at slavery from within. By making slaves the main characters of her novel *Uncle Tom's Cabin*, Stowe forced her readers to see the slaves as humans who had the same feelings and struggles as them.

For example, with the character of Eliza, Stowe allowed women to feel the horrors of having a child torn from you and sold to another family.

Stowe was so successful in stirring the emotions of her readers many credited her with being one of the major instigators of the Civil War. In fact legend has it that in meeting Stowe, Lincoln said "So you're the little woman who wrote the book that started this great war."[9] She clearly shows us that justice must begin from within. Like Lewis, she challenges us to look at how our actions affect individuals. She gives us reason to look beyond the arguments of profit, unity, progress and development that might mislead us and distract us as we attempt to justify our actions. To consider the virtue of our actions, both Stowe and Lewis advise to look within.

Finding Purpose

In what roles are you most likely to look for external justifications for your actions? Why?

What would be the affect of your looking within to assess your actions? What would be the reactions of others working with you? Why?

Which actions does this scene cause you to reflect on? What do you find when you look within rather than outward as you assess and reflect on your actions? Who do your actions affect personally? How might you change your actions to consider the humanity of these people?

Finding Scripture

In the New Testament, we find where Lewis and Stowe find their Christian teachings. In calling the Pharisees and Sadducees laws and practices into question, we find him urging them to look beyond an obedience to law in finding and delivering justice. While there are many examples of this, I find John's account of Jesus saving the woman from stoning as a telling paradigm of how we are to work for justice. You will recall that the Pharisees brought a woman who had been accused of adultery to Jesus and asked his opinion of Moses's command to stone women guilty of such a sin. While they were deliberately setting a trap for him and expecting him to blindly uphold the law, Jesus forced them instead to look within themselves to find the just treatment of the woman. He commands for the one who has not sinned to cast the first stone at her. Of course, none of them could make such a claim—as they had all been guilty of sin. What is remarkable here is that Jesus puts a face on sin and judgment. He looks at the individual person rather than the overarching, external law. He calls us to look within ourselves before we act. Thus, he makes justice very personal and human.

Suggested Scripture Reading and Reflections

Read John 8: 1-11, then use the following questions to reflect on how the reading is calling to you reflect on your own actions and call to justice.

Why do you think Jesus writes on the ground after he is asked about what to do with the woman? What does this mean for us?

What laws do you use to justify actions that you aren't comfortable with? How does Jesus model justice for us? How would he define justice? Why is Jesus's notion of justice more challenging than the Pharisees? Whose ideas of justice do you model—the Pharisees or Jesus'?

In which role, might Jesus be calling you to reform your actions and to act more justly? How will you respond?

How did he ask the woman to look within? The Pharisees? You?

DELIVERING GRACE TO THE UNGRACIOUS

REFLECTIONS ON LEWIS'S VOYAGE

Before Eustace had his transformation as a dragon, he acted rather beastly to his cousins and the members of the Dawn Treader. You probably also remember that at the start of the voyage in addition to being very rude, he was also very sea sick. While we might at first see his sickness as being a just reward for his behavior, Lewis causes us to reflect on this type of thinking when we are told that "Lucy's conscience smote her"[10] and then we hear her say "I think I really must go and see Eustace."[11] She pulls herself away from the excitement of seeing the ship and goes to the aid of her cousin, Eustace. And when questioned by Caspian as to whether or not her magical potion "ought to be wasted on a thing like seasickness"[12] (and perhaps we also wonder if it should be wasted on such an ungracious and rude boy like Eustace), Lucy immediately responds "It'll only take a drop."[13] Lucy doesn't judge who or when the magical, healing potion should be used. Instead, she administers it freely to all—regardless of the situation and the person. And this is likely why Aslan gave the potion to her to administer. He knew her heart and trusted she would share it justly.

This scene teaches us an important lesson, as most of us would have thought along the lines of Caspian. We would have questioned if the situation and person really deserved the healing potion. I believe Lewis uses this scene to illustrate a point that he also makes in *Christian Behaviour* where he reminds us that the New Testament tells us that "every one must work ... 'in order to give to those in need.'"[14] And in elaborating further on this point, he brings to our attention the common argument often made that "instead of giving to the poor we ought to be producing a society in which there were no poor to give."[15] And while he agrees that "we ought to produce that kind of society," it does not excuse us from "giving in the meantime."[16] He then explains that using this type of reasoning to excuse ourselves from giving reveals a turning away from "Christian Morality."[17] And in determining how much we should give, he says "the only safe rule is to give more than we can spare."[18]

And while Lewis's reading of Scripture may seem idealistic and tough to follow, in looking at his own life, you will find that he took these Christian teachings to heart. Many examples of this diligence have been shared by his brother, friends, and stepson. For example, Warren tells us in the introduction of *Letters of C. S. Lewis*, that upon receiving his first real monetary success with his publication of *The Screwtape Letters*, "he celebrated by a lavish and improvident scattering of cheques to various societies and individual lame dogs."[19] And later, "a charitable trust was set up into which two-thirds of his royalties was thereafter paid automatically."[20] Warren also shares that this was only one example of his charity. For "over and above this, he had in an extraordinary degree the deeper charity that can perhaps best be described as a universal and sympathetic neighborliness to all and sundry, strangers, as well as acquaintances."[21]

Personal Ponderings

I have to admit that through this scene, his explanation of charity, and his example in living, Lewis humbles me and challenges me. I can recall several occasions where I have fallen prey to the type of thinking that Lewis shows to be of unChristian sentiment. I often attempt to rationalize why I shouldn't give with the exact reasoning that Lewis touches upon. Rather that remembering that Jesus calls us to give freely and unconditionally, I look at the situation through the reasoning of society: *I would only be enabling that person. He or she needs to face their natural consequences so that this won't happen again. Surely, he or she is only reaping what was sown. I have had to fend for myself; she or he should also.* Certainly have you heard this thinking and perhaps even voiced some of it yourself. But Lewis reminds us here that the call to charity is not conditional. We are not the ones to judge who should or should not be helped. God gives to us and blesses us so that we may give to others. What he gives to us is not ours to keep but to give.

As I write this, I am reminded of a scene from the movie *Jerry McGuire*. In one of the more motivating scenes between McGuire and his friend and client Rod Tidwell, we see McGuire frustrated that Tidwell continues to dwell on who isn't giving him attention, who unjustly is getting more than him, and "who isn't showing [him] the money." McGuire, finally hearing enough, blows up and forces Tidwell to listen to himself. He ends the conversation by saying Tidwell's constant complaining and focus on what he isn't receiving "doesn't inspire people!" And couldn't this also be said of our own rationalizing about why we shouldn't give and share with others? In our judgmental and escapist attitudes and actions aren't we forgetting what led us to Christianity in the first place? Refusing to listen to the heart of our faith, are we missing out on the chance to "inspire people"?

Finding Purpose

When have you rationalized and made excuses for not helping someone in need? Which excuses do you rely on most? Why is it easier for us to rely on the attitudes of society than on our Christian faith? Why do we find it so difficult to give? How can work on changing our attitudes to be more "inspiring"?

Finding Scripture

In the New Testament, we see the Pharisees and Sadducees finding multiple reasons why they should not accept Jesus as the Messiah or believe in the miracles that he performs. Even Jesus's disciples fall prey to this type of thinking from time to time. Like us, they clung to their human attitudes and to the ways of this world. In their reasoning and justifications, I fear we often find our own sinful attitudes and reasoning—which prevents us from fully embracing Jesus's teaching. But if we are to receive eternal life, we need to change our attitudes and our hearts. John gives us a chance to reflect on our thinking and attitudes about faith when he shares how Jesus opened the eyes of a man who had been born blind.

Upon approaching the man, the disciples are not really drawn to help the man. Like others passing by the poor beggar, they do not think of how they might help him. Rather they embrace our society's type of thinking, as they ask Jesus if the man was blind because of his own sins or the sins of his parents. Jesus tells them neither. The man was not born blind because of sin. Jesus explains that the man was born blind so that God's works might be made visible to others. He then heals the man and restores the man's sight.

We then hear the Pharisees echo our worldly reasoning as they refuse to believe that Jesus is doing God's work. They reason that he performed a miracle on the Sabbath, which Moses forbade. They reason that a man breaking Moses's law must be sinful and could not do the work of God. They then question the man's parents to verify that the man was really born blind. In finding that he was, they question the man again about what happened, and then they reason that it must have been a hoax—that the man was really a disciple of Jesus.

Suggested Scripture Reading and Reflections

Read John 9: 1-11, then use the following questions to reflect on how well you model your Christian faith.

Why did the disciples immediately assume that the blind man had sinned or that his parents had sinned? How is this attitude prevalent in today's society? Why do we make these assumptions?

Why did the Pharisees refuse to believe? How would you have responded?

How does Jesus address this type of reasoning? How does this reading speak to you? What is it calling you to do?

Learning to Listen

Reflections on Lewis's Voyage

After Eustace is unscaled as a dragon and redressed as a boy by Aslan, Lewis chooses to have Eustace first share his experience with Edmund. This is significant because Edmund had also had a similar experience with Aslan. Both had sinned and both had been forgiven. This made their conversation confessional. It also signifies the need for us experience healing through telling our failings to another person who has also failed and can understand. Edmund was able to understand Eustace's feelings because he had also failed. You will remember that in *The Lion, the Witch, and the Wardrobe*, Edmund betrayed his siblings to the White Witch. But Aslan forgave Edmund and allowed him to put his failings in the past and move forward. Thus, when Eustace says "And by the way, I'd like to apologize. I'm afraid I've been beastly."[22] Edmund is able to listen openly and to offer understanding and forgiveness, as he responds "That's all right. Between ourselves, you haven't been as bad as I was on my first trip to Narnia. You were only an ass, but I was a traitor."[23]

In this short and sincere scene between the two boys, Lewis depicts what he means by the Christian commandment of loving your neighbor as yourself. In reflecting on our call to forgiveness as Christians, Lewis tells us that loving ourselves calls us to look at both our "nice" actions and "nasty" actions so that we might also understand others' failings and regret their failings in the same way that we regret our own.[24] And in that same reasoning, in understanding their failings with our own, we should also hope as we hope for ourselves "that somehow, sometime, somewhere, he can be cured and made human again."[25] And when that transformation does occur, we might rejoice. And that is exactly what the crew of the *Dawn Tread-*

er did. As Eustace and Edmund walked toward the camp fire, Lewis tells us "great was the rejoicing."[26]

Personal Ponderings

It seems that Lewis is teaching us in this scene that listening is linked with forgiveness. In learning to forgive, we must also learn to listen. And in listening, we must open our hearts and hear with our own failings. This allows us to enter into the conversation with an attitude of empathy and compassion. In listening to our own failings, we humbly listen to our neighbors' failings and find ourselves. We see that we are connected and must help one another. For in each others' successes, we find our own.

This Christian calling challenges us. It is not easy to listen and to forgive. Nor is it easy to reflect on our own failings, but when we do—we can change. Martin Luther King, Jr. inspired this type of change. He brought people together regardless of color, race, and ethnicity. He inspired people to look beyond the hurts of the past and to instead see each other as humans bound together in a common cause that could only be improved by understanding and loving one another. His famous "I Have a Dream" speech continues to inspire us to listen to the needs of each other when he says "Now is the time to lift our nation from the quick sands of racial injustice to the solid rock of brotherhood. Now is the time to make justice a reality for all of God's children."[27] Notice that he does not only mention justice for African Americans, he shows that injustice for anyone threatens the justice of all "God's children." In dreaming that one day, "little black boys and black girls will be able to join hands with little white boys and white girls as sisters and brothers,"[28] he calls us to look beyond the past, beyond appearances, beyond hurts, and to listen to one another as fellow human beings so that in the future we can forgive, rejoice, and work for goodness and justice for each other. In essence, like Lewis, King is showing us that we can love our neighbors as ourselves. But we must be willing to hope, dream, forgive, and truly listen to each other. For if we don't learn to listen to each other and love one another in this way, Lewis predicts "we shall be fixed for ever in a universe of pure hatred."[29]

Finding Purpose

When do you find it most difficult to listen to someone? How does this scene challenge your understanding of listening? When has someone listened to you as Edmund listened to Eustace? What was the result? Who really needs you to listen to him or her right now? Why? Who do you need to listen to you? How does God's promise of reconciliation invite this type of listening? What makes this type of listening so difficult? How might it bring about social change if everyone were to listen in this way?

Finding Scripture

Lewis and King both show us that in order to truly listen to one another we need to approach one another with humility. We must look first to our own failings before we can listen to each other. This lesson also comes to us in Scripture in the parable of the Pharisee and the tax collector. While most might assume that a tax collector would be far from Christlike, Jesus shows us that the tax collector embraces the attitude of humility that we also must embrace. And in helping us to understand how to love our neighbor as ourselves to work for justice, Jesus offers us the Parable of the Good Samaritan.

Suggested Scripture Reading and Reflections

Read the two parables Jesus offers us (Luke 10:25-37; Luke 18:9-14), and then use the questions below to further reflect on what the two parables tell us about the kind of attitude we must have as we listen to one another and learn to love each other.

What was different about the Pharisee's attitude and the tax collector's attitude? Which person would be a better listener? Why? What would keep one from truly listening to others? Why does Jesus offer us this parable? How does it speak to you?

Which attitude does the priest reflect? The Levite? The Samaritan? How does this attitude contribute to social justice? What does it tell us about humility, listening, and loving others?

CALLED TO SERVE

REFLECTIONS ON LEWIS'S VOYAGE

In *Beyond Personality*, Lewis discusses an aspect of service that most of us may never really think about on our own. He believes that in serving God—in looking for him—we actually find ourselves. He says that "the very first step is to try to forget about the self altogether,"[30] which would mean thinking and focusing on others' needs. And in getting "'ourselves' out of the way" the "more truly ourselves we become."[31] He argues that this happens because when we forget ourselves and help others we allow God to take over and work through us. And thus, we find our true personality.

Lewis gives us a hint of this through Lucy. You will remember that she insisted on helping the invisible people even when the others believed she shouldn't. And then when she finally does go on her own into the house to help find the spell to make the invisible people visible again, we find her undergoing some personal struggles. She comes across a spell that tempts her with knowledge of what her friends have said about her. And she also wrestles with her jealousy of Susan's beauty. In the midst of this, she meets Aslan who puts her back on track. And, she soon finds the spell to help the invisible people.

But what seems to be key to the scene is Lucy's internal struggles that are released during her act of helping others. And in those struggles she found Aslan and was able to overcome them and leave the house of the magician a much stronger and less selfish person. So, here in this scene, Lewis uses Lucy to demonstrate what he explained in *Beyond Personality* and perhaps had experienced himself. When we help others, we actually help ourselves. But ironically, we can only truly come to know ourselves when we forget ourselves in the act of serving others. Lewis tells us that this "principal runs through all life.... Give up yourself, and you'll find your real self."³²

PERSONAL PONDERINGS

Lewis presents us with another one of the tough Christian challenges here. While we may claim to give of ourselves often, to give in the way that Jesus modeled is not easy. Jesus completely gave himself over so that we might have eternal life. And even though the thought of giving in this way may terrify us, some of the saints took this call to serve to heart. In fact, Saint Francis of Assisi provides us with an example of someone who not only gave of himself but also found himself in doing so.

Francis was born in 1182 into a wealthy home. And as he entered his teens, he often spent his riches freely. He spent his time spending, eating, and partying. He was also very attractive and sought after by many eligible women, but he none of this really fulfilled him. Looking for more, he joined the army in hopes of becoming knight when Assisi declared war on Perugia.

During the battle, Assisi was overtaken by Perugia and wealthy warriors were captured and held for ransom. After a year, he was released and soon went back to his partying. Again, looking for fulfillment, Francis joined in the battle of the Fourth Crusade hoping to return a prince. But several strange encounters began to awaken Francis to his call to serve God and others. On one occasion, he met a poor man to whom he gave his cloak. On another, he met a leper, who he approached and kissed—finding himself to receive a kiss of peace. He also had dreams and heard a voice ask him "to repair my church."

Francis believed these encounters to be from God—and he responded by giving up his riches and family name. In fact, his father denounced him and sued him for the riches he gave to a church. But by giving up all the material possessions he had and in devoting himself to the service and God and others, Francis found himself. He finally found happiness and fulfillment, for the first time fully feeling a true brotherhood with humanity and a connection with God's creation. Francis was known for not only preaching God's word to humans but to animals as well. He found his call to serve not only people—but all of God's creation.[33]

And like the example with Lucy, Francis began to grapple with and find himself when he was not thinking of himself. When he began to serve others, he found himself.

Finding Purpose

When have you found yourself while serving others? What did you discover about yourself?

Why is hard to let go of ourselves even after we have found happiness in serving others?

Who is God calling you to serve now? How will you respond?

Finding Scripture

In reading Paul's letters to the Phillippians, we find that he also found and taught the same lessons that Lewis and Francis shared with us. For example, in Phillippians 3:12-16, Paul tells us that he has been completely possessed by Christ. And in allowing Jesus to control his thoughts, words, moods, and actions, he has found a new attitude—an attitude that has brought him peace, happiness and cause for rejoicing. Like Lucy and Francis, by letting go of himself, Paul found himself. And in that transformation, he found lasting peace and happiness. And like Francis, Paul also found this only in completely giving up his worldly gains (Phillippian 3: 7, 19-20).

In Phillippians 4:4-9, he tells us how we can also find ourselves. He also advises us to think of and cling only to those things that are honorable, just, pure, lovely, and gracious. In other words, he shows us what it means to serve God and others. He helps us to understand the true meaning of justice.

Suggested Scripture Reading and Reflections

Read Phillippians 4:4-9, and then use the questions below to reflect on how God is calling you and how in serving you might find yourself transformed and experience lasting peace and happiness.

Paul tells us that if we rejoice in the Lord our kindness will be known to all? What do you think he means by this? How is he linking rejoice with service here?

How do you rejoice in the Lord? How does this allow you to show kindness to others?

How does God help you to discern what is honorable, just, true, pure, lovely, and gracious? How does the material world lead us astray? How did Francis avoid this? Paul? Lewis? How can we avoid the distractions of the material world so that we can allow God to work through us?

WISE COUNSEL

REFLECTIONS ON LEWIS'S VOYAGE

Once the Caspian and his crew reach the end of the world, he realizes that Reepicheep will soon be gone and that Lucy, Edmund and Eustace will also soon return to their world. This causes him great sadness and leads him to proclaim that he will sail on with Reepicheep and let his crew sail home alone without him. This creates great alarm and stir from everyone. Edmund tells him "You can't do this."[34] And Reepicheep concurs "Most certainly, his majesty cannot."[35] This is echoed by Drinian who says "No indeed."[36] And Rynelf reminds him that he cannot place himself above the law. If one of them acted in the same manner, "it would be called deserting."[37]

Caspian becomes angry at their reactions and attempts to quiet them by reminding them that he is the king, and thus he can do as he pleases. But Reepicheep wisely counsels him that it is because he is the King of Narnia that he cannot simply do as he pleases. He tells Caspian, "You are the King of Narnia. You will break faith with all your subjects, and especially Trumpkin, if you do not return. You shall not please yourself with adventures as if you were a private person."[38]

Here, Lewis uses Reepicheep to remind us that moral law is not subjective to our own situations and pleasures—regardless of our position. And Caspian later comes to this realization later when he takes time to reflect and listen to his conscience. In reflecting, he hears Aslan tell him what he already knew to be true and just. Aslan tells him that he must allow the others "to go on," and he must "go back."[39]

Lewis speaks openly and candidly about this struggle with situational ethics in *Christian Reflections* where he says that those who believe they can create their own conscience and hold themselves to their own notion of what is good will eventually realize "that those who create conscience cannot be subject to conscience themselves"[40] and that this notion allows rulers "to stand above and outside his own creation." And in understanding this, we, like Lewis, come to the realization that "Subjectivism about values is eternally incompatible with democracy." Allowing ourselves and our leaders to act as though we or they are separate from the rest of our community will cause all of us to "perish."[41]

Personal Ponderings

Here, Lewis shows us how we might easily be led astray in our causes by allowing ourselves to form our own idea of good and just. If we don't hold ourselves and others accountable to a greater overarching moral law, our subjectivity defeats the purpose of democracy. As we look back through history, we can cite many examples where this has been the case. In convincing Germany that persecuting the Jews was for the greater good of the country, Hitler fashioned his own distorted version of moral law. By allowing Hitler to subjectively determine the value of human life, Germany allowed genocide to flourish—which brought about World War II.

So how do we determine moral law? Lewis notes that moral law is not new or created. He says "The good is uncreated." [42] And in establishing this claim, he points to:

> ... massive unanimity of the practical reason in man. From the Babylonian Hymn to Samos, from the Laws of Manu, the Book of the Dead, the Analects, the Stoics, the Platonists from Australian aborigines and Redskins, [you] will collect the same triumphantly monotonous denunciations of oppression, murder, treachery and falsehood, the same injunctions of kindness to the aged, the young, and the weak, of almsgiving and impartiality and honesty.[43]

As Christians, we recognize this as the Golden Rule, tor to love others as we love ourselves. As I mentioned earlier, Stephen Covey is known for naming this universal moral law True North. And as discussed in a previous section, he says that to find this inner moral compass we must take time to reflect and to listen—as Lewis showed Caspian doing. In *First Things First,* Covey tells us that "The power to create quality of life is within us—in our ability to develop and use our own inner compass so that we can act with integrity in the moment of choice."[44]

And while we may readily nod our heads and agree with all of this, we often find it much more complex when we—like Caspian—are faced with that moment of choice. We quickly wonder what our inner compass is really telling us. And in that moment, we could easily be convinced that what we want to do is in fact what our compass is telling us to do. This is where it becomes important to remove ourselves from the world. We must take on "a sense of humility" and accept, as Caspian had to in the scene discussed above, that "We're not in control of our own lives; principles are." When we are able to find peace in that, "We cease trying to be a law unto ourselves…. We become involved in an ongoing quest to understand and live in harmony with the laws of life."[45]

Finding Purpose

When have you felt justified in making your own rules? What was the response of others around you? How did you respond? If you would have listened to your inner compass or conscience, what would have told you?

Have you noticed that losing a sense of humility results in an attitude that leads one to act outside the laws of Nature? What makes it difficult to adhere to a common moral law? What arguments does the world use to deny a moral law? Why? How do you respond?

Finding Scripture

In Matthew 5, Jesus gives us a common moral law to follow. Here, we find his famous Sermon on the Mount, which reiterates the necessity of humility. He not only tells us that we are called to serve others, but he also tells us that we should do it in private so that not even our right hand knows what the left is doing.

Suggested Scripture Reading and Reflections

As you read Matthew 5, notice how Jesus's teachings parallel teachings of all humanity and religions, yet seem contrary to the teachings of our material world. Then use the questions below for further reflection.

How do Jesus's teachings reflect universal moral teachings? How are they contrary to the teachings of our material world? Why do you think humility is so important? So difficult? While you may have read The Sermon on the Mount many times before, what really seemed to speak to you this time? Why? How did reading it in conjunction with this section of the book allow you to find some new meaning in the Scripture reading?

Leaving No One Behind

Reflections on Lewis's Voyage

While in the beginning of the journey, Eustace seemed nothing but trouble for the crew of the *Dawn Treader*. Lewis shows us that the crew continued to respect and look after him even when it was as Caspian described a "nuisance" and "endless trouble."[46] When he wandered off, they looked for him, and Lucy worried for his safety. Even Reepicheep, who had wanted to fight him, argued to Rhince that despite Eustace's bad behavior and the crew's negative feelings toward Eustace "it concerns our honor to find him and to avenge him if he is dead."[47]

And once they discovered that he had been turned into a dragon, instead of leaving him behind on the island they pondered ways of how they would bring him along—despite the problems of not being able to fit him on the ship. They never even consider leaving without him. What Lewis shows us here is essentially what he calls "Let's Pretend" in *Beyond Personality*.[48] In his essay (broadcast talk), Lewis gives us the example of Beauty and the Beast to show how as Christians we can learn to love others and love them as ourselves by pretending that they are good—or perhaps treating them as they are Christ. We can also act as though we are Christ—or the Son of God. In this sense, we are pretending. We are putting on the costume of Christ and acting as he would—and envisioning those we are helping to be dressed as Christ. Why? Because essentially, Christianity tells us that we are Christ. He resides in each of us. As Lewis aptly puts it "Men are mirrors, or 'carriers' of Christ to other men. Sometimes unconscious men."[49] So in deciding how to treat someone, his or her past or current actions become irrelevant—all that really matters is that Christ resides in him and us. And pretending to act as though we were Christ, clothing ourselves in his actions, may "lead up to the real thing."[50]

As Lewis explains, "Very often the only way to get a quality in reality is to start behaving as you have it already."[51]

The crew moves beyond their negative feelings for Eustace by pretending that he really is the nice and kind boy that he could be. They think of him as a human or a crew member rather than as the Eustace they have (in some cases, with regret) come to know—or wish they didn't know, as may be the case. Reepicheep voices this sentiment when he argues to Rhince and the crew that "he is one of our fellowship." And the outcome in the story is favorable. As a result of their kindness, Eustace eventually becomes the boy and the crew member they envisioned him to be. By refusing to leave him behind, they helped Aslan to transform him, and they allowed themselves to be transformed.

Personal Ponderings

Lewis's concept of pretending here reminds me of how literature has been instrumental for me as a teacher and parent. Often times I find that literature opens windows for us to imagine ourselves as others—to allow ourselves and others to imagine what it might be like to walk in someone else's shoes. For example, while reading Harry Potter, I can imagine what it would be like to be an orphan in a home where I am not welcome or loved. How many other children must feel the same way? Or, I can imagine myself as a student facing constant ridicule from a teacher who does not like me or even want to teach me. Additionally, I can get a glimpse of how it feels to live with post-traumatic stress syndrome, where flashbacks and pain may force themselves upon me at any moment in time causing me anxiety, stress, and feelings of impending doom. While the story is fictional, the situations are very real. And in associating with the character, I begin to feel the reality of the situation. I begin to understand others whom I interact with in new ways. And, in finding similarities with my own life, I find healing as I hear others talk about the characters and begin to understand my plight.

Entering fictional worlds where we pretend to be others allows us to pretend in the real world, as Lewis suggests. It allows us to imagine ourselves as others—and as Christians it allows us to more easily envision acting as a son or daughter of God would act. And in pretending, we may find that when we take off our masks and costumes we are transformed. Like Eustace, we may find that we no longer are dragons.

Finding Purpose

Who do you find it most difficult to help? Why? How might it help if you envision him or her as Christ? How might it help if you envision yourself as Christ? How would your actions be different?

Finding Scripture

In Genesis 18, we find God's patience and desire to save and rescue even amidst sin. When God tells Abraham of his plan to punish Sodom for their sin, Abraham asks God repeatedly if he will punish the innocent with the guilty. Not only does God show patience with Abraham's questioning, he also tells Abraham that he will not destroy Sodom if there is a possibility for good. If any innocent are present, he will hold off punishment. Read Genesis 18:22-33 and then use the questions below to reflect on God's patience and desire to leave no one behind.

Suggested Scripture Reading and Reflections

Why do you think Abraham questions God repeatedly? How does he represent our own way of thinking and questioning of God?

When have you questioned God repeatedly? Why? How did God respond with the same type of patience?

What does God's willingness and desire to save teach us? If we are to dress ourselves as sons and daughters of God, what does this Scripture reading reveal to us about how we are to treat others? What does this teach us about justice?

Delivering from Danger

Reflections on Lewis's Voyage

When Caspian pulls Lord Rhoop out of the dark waters and rescues him from the dark island, Lewis gives us a chance to reflect on how we might also rescue others and deliver them from danger. If you remember, before they find Lord Rhoop, the crew is tempted to turn around and avoid the darkness when Caspian asks "Do we go into this?"[52] But Reepicheep quickly intervenes and tells them that any "suggestion" of turning around and leaving "proceeded from cowardice."[53]

Through Reepicheep's refusal to turn back and the crew's success in rescuing Lord Rhoop, Lewis gives us a tangible example of the feelings we may encounter when faced with the challenge of Christianity. As Christians working for justice, we may face very real and difficult situations that frighten us. And we may feel that the task is beyond us. We may even convince ourselves that turning back would be the wisest decision for all involved. But as Lewis tells us in *Beyond Personality* and shows us here in this scene, Christ demands that we give him our entire self to work through. And in giving God ourselves, we come to realize that " 'morality' or 'decent behaviour' or 'the good of society'—has claims on this self: claims which interfere with its own desires."[54] And while the task before us might seem impossible, like sailing into complete darkness blindly, our call to justice and relinquishing our self to Christ pushes us to ignore the selfish desires of the world. That is usually where we meet fear and find ourselves asking as Caspian did "Do we go into this?" That is also where we need to remember that to push forward we must stop thinking as "if it were *we* who did everything."[55] And remember: "In reality, of course, it is God who does everything."[56] We must empty our desires and turn ourselves over to him to allow him to work in us and through us. Then, no task will be impossible, for God desires to pull others to him and deliver them from danger and injustice. We just need to allow him to do his work. Like Caspian and the crew of the *Dawn Treader*, we may find ourselves sailing blindly into darkness—but in that darkness we may also find our mission and the ability to help others.

Finding Purpose

Recently while watching the movie *Hotel Rwanda*, I saw hotel manager Paul Rusesabagina (portrayed by actor Don Cheadle) model what Lewis describes and depicts. When the Hutu militants began to massacre the Tutsis in Rwanda in 1994, Rusesabagina found himself and his family herded onto a bus by the Hutu militants. Being a mixture of Hutu and Tutsi, he faced great danger of being killed with the other Tutsis who the Hutus referred to as cockroaches. To test his loyalty, they gave him a gun and instructed him to kill all of the cockroaches on the bus.

Here is the moment where fear must have consumed him. But as he was faced with the question Caspian voiced "Do we go into this?" he looked into the faces of fellow humans and decided he could not kill. Instead, he quickly thought of a way to save. Being a manager of two hotels, he had access to resources that most did not. So he appealed to the militants' greed and offered them money. He asked them to drive him to the Hotel Diplomate where he could open the safe and give them cash. His only request was that he spare the lives of those on the bus. Judging his captors correctly, they complied. After receiving their cash, Rusesabinga drove the bus and everyone on it to Hotel des Milles Collines where he created a safe haven for Tutsis. Despite many challenges from cut off water supply, cut phone lines and violent attacks, he was able to maintain the safety of over 1200 Tutsis—when over 8,000 were killed daily outside the hotel.[57]

In letting go of himself, Rusesabinga allowed God to work through him. In his actions, he shows us that if we let go of our own selfish desires and wants, God can work through us to help others and to achieve what may seem impossible. Often, this results in helping bring justice to others in need. As Lewis aptly explained "Men are mirrors or 'carriers' of Christ to other men. Sometimes unconscious carriers. This 'good infection' can be carried by those who haven't got it themselves. People who weren't Christians helped me to Christianity."[58]

Finding Purpose

When have you found yourself afraid of helping someone else? What were you afraid of? Why? What was the outcome? When have you allowed God to work through you? How did you get beyond the fear? What was the result? When has God helped you through someone else?

How can you become better at letting go of your selfish desires and fears to let God work through you? How might living moment by moment make the task easier?

Finding Scripture

In Exodus, Moses finds himself facing what he believes to be the impossible. God has asked him to go to the Pharaoh of Egypt and let the Israelites go free. Believing himself to be a poor speaker and also being in exile from the country, Moses has some serious fears. But God assures him that the task is not impossible. He only needs to allow God to work through him. Letting go of his fears, Moses allows God to perform many miracles and free the Israelites. Here, in Scripture we find the original source of the message that Lewis learned and shows us in his writings.

Suggested Scripture Reading and Reflections

After reading Exodus 6—12, use the following questions to reflect on how God wants to work through you to achieve justice for others.

Why does Moses question his ability to help the Israelites? When have you used your lack of abilities as an excuse not to help someone? What was the result?

How does God overcome Moses's fears? How might he help you overcome your fear?

Who is God calling you to help? How are you responding?

CLOSING THOUGHTS

Re-visiting the Narnia series as an adult has reminded me that you are never too old to dream and imagine. Lewis who spent most of his young-adult life arguing that God does not exist found God in his adult life and became one of the most prolific Christian writers. Among his publications, his Narnia series continues to be his most famous and attracts audiences both young and old. While some of his readers may not be aware of Lewis' intentions or Lewis's struggles, the series will undoubtedly lead them into the realm of imagination. In this realm, we learn to believe in things that we cannot see, feel, touch, smell, or taste. This is the same realm where we find God.

This is the beauty of literature and the arts. They allow us to feel, dream, envision, and create; they allow us to imagine. And in imagining, we often enter the spiritual realm where good and evil compete for our allegiance. In Narnia, Lewis takes us on a voyage to an imaginary world where we discover ourselves, our struggles, and our faith, as he shows us why we should align ourselves with good—so that we, like Reepicheep who sailed into Aslan's Country, may be reunited with our God in his heavenly kingdom.

Endnotes

Section One

[1] C.S. Lewis, *Christian Behaviour* (New York: The Macmillan Company, 1944), 7–8.
[2] C.S. Lewis, *The Chronicles of Narnia* (New York: HarperCollins Publishers, 2001), 456–458.
[3] C.S. Lewis, *Surprised by Joy: The Shape of my Early Life* (New York: A Harvest Book, Harcourt Inc., 1955), 116.
[4] C.S. Lewis, *The Chronicles of Narnia* (New York: HarperCollins Publishers, 2001), 460.
[5] Walter Hooper, ed., They Stand Together: The Letters of C.S. Lewis to Arthur Greeves (1914–1963) (New York: Macmillan Publishing Company, 1979), 217.
[6] Ibid, 214.
[7] Ibid, 217.
[8] Ibid, 217.
[9] Ibid, 221.
[10] Ibid, 203.
[11] Ibid, 235.
[12] Helen Keller, *The Story of My Life*, (New York: Signet Classics, 2002), 6–7.
[13] Ibid, 8.
[14] Ibid, 16.
[15] Ibid, 17.
[16] Ibid, 18.
[17] Ibid, 19.
[18] Ibid.
[19] Ibid, 21.
[20] Ibid, 24.
[21] C.S. Lewis, *The Chronicles of Narnia* (New York: HarperCollins Publishers, 2001), 478.
[22] Ibid, 479.
[23] Ibid, 478.
[24] W.H. Lewis, ed., *Letters of C.S. Lewis* (London: The Chaucer Press, 1966), 9.
[25] Walter Hooper, ed., *They Stand Together: The Letters of C.S. Lewis to Arthur Greeves (1914–1963)* (New York: Macmillan Publishing Company, 1979), 258.

26 W.H. Lewis, ed., *Letters of C.S. Lewis* (London: The Chaucer Press, 1966), 10.
27 Walter Hooper, ed., *They Stand Together: The Letters of C.S. Lewis to Arthur Greeves (1914-1963)* (New York: Macmillan Publishing Company, 1979), 258.
28 Ibid, 260.
29 W.H. Lewis, ed., *Letters of C.S. Lewis* (London: The Chaucer Press, 1966), 137.
30 Ibid, 139.
31 Walter Hooper, ed., *They Stand Together: The Letters of C.S. Lewis to Arthur Greeves (1914-1963)* (New York: Macmillan Publishing Company, 1979), 102.
32 Gandhian Institution Bombay Sorvodaya Ma, "Chronology," *A Comprehensive Site*, May 22, 2008, http://www.mkgandhi-sarvodaya.org/under.htm.
33 Ibid.
34 *Great Lives Great Deeds* (Pleasantville, New York: The Reader's Digest Association, 1964), 120-21.
35 Gandhian Institution Bombay Sorvodaya Ma, "Peace, Nonviolence, and Conflict Resolution," 452, *A Comprehensive Site*, May 22, 2008, http://www.mkgandhi-sarvodaya.org/nonvio/index.htm.
36 Mahatma Gandhi, *The Story of My Experiments with Truth*, "Acquaintance with Religions, Part 1, Chapter XX," (Nalanda Digital Library), May 23, 2008, http://www.nalanda.nitc.ac.in/resources/english/etext-project/biography/gandhi/
37 Sherwood Eliot Wirt, "C. S. Lewis on Heaven, Earth, and Outer Space," interview by Sherwood Eliot Wirt, Assist News Service, May 7, 1963, http://www.cbn.com/special/Narnia/articles/ans_LewisLastInterviewB.aspx (accessed April 25, 2008).
38 C.S. Lewis, *The Chronicles of Narnia* (New York: HarperCollins Publishers, 2001), 482.
39 Ibid.
40 Ibid.
41 Tara Parker-Pope, "A Hint of Hope as Obesity Rates Hit Plateau," *New York Times* (May 28, 2008), http://www.nytimes.com/2008/05/28/health/research/28obesity.html?_r=1&th&emc=th&oref=slogin
42 Ibid.
43 C.S. Lewis, *The Chronicles of Narnia* (New York: HarperCollins Publishers, 2001), 506.

⁴⁴ C.S. Lewis, *Surprised by Joy: The Shape of my Early Life* (New York: A Harvest Book, Harcourt Inc., 1955), 51.
⁴⁵ George Bailey, "Chapter Four: In the University," in *C. S. Lewis Speaker and Teacher,* ed. Carolyn Keefe, 79-92 (Grand Rapids Michigan: Zondervan Publishing House, 1971), 85.
⁴⁶ C.S. Lewis, *Surprised by Joy: The Shape of my Early Life* (New York: A Harvest Book, Harcourt Inc., 1955), 64.
⁴⁷ Ibid.
⁴⁸ Ibid.
⁴⁹ Ibid, 65.
⁵⁰ Ibid.
⁵¹ Ibid, 65-66.
⁵² C.S. Lewis, *The Chronicles of Narnia* (New York: HarperCollins Publishers, 2001), 509.
⁵³ C.S. Lewis, *Surprised by Joy: The Shape of my Early Life* (New York: A Harvest Book, Harcourt Inc., 1955), 68.
⁵⁴ Ibid, 107.
⁵⁵ Ibid, 108.
⁵⁶ C.S. Lewis, *The Chronicles of Narnia* (New York: HarperCollins Publishers, 2001), 508.
⁵⁷ C.S. Lewis, *Surprised by Joy: The Shape of my Early Life* (New York: A Harvest Book, Harcourt Inc., 1955), 109.
⁵⁸ Roger Lancelyn Green, "In the Evening," in *C. S. Lewis at the Breakfast Table and Other Reminiscences,* ed. James T. Como, 210-214 (New York: Macmillan Publishing Co., Inc., 1979), 213. *They Stand Together: The Letters of C.S. Lewis to Arthur Greeves (1914-1963)*
⁵⁹ Walter Hooper, ed., (New York: Macmillan Publishing Company, 1979), 111.
⁶⁰ Associated Press, "Iowa tornado rated state's strongest in 32 years," (May 28, 2008) http://ap.google.com/article/ALeqM5iMxAxJ-Orfj5UrRL2NjxzG_4-TrAD90U8B5O0
⁶¹ Grant Schulte, "Iowans Pick Through Tornado Disaster Area," *USA Today* (May 28, 2008) http://www.usatoday.com/weather/storms/2008-05-27-iowa_tornado_loss_N.htm?csp=34
⁶² Ibid.
⁶³ "Tornadoes of 2008: Neighbors Helping Neighbors - you did an incredible job!," KWWL.com (May 30, 2008) http://www.kwwl.com/Global/category.asp?C=128859&nav=menu82_1
⁶⁴ "Salvation Army's Tornado Relief Efforts," KWWL.com (May 30, 2008) http://www.kwwl.com/global/story.asp?s=8400441

[65] "USDA Rural Development Offers Housing to Tornado Survivors," KWWL.com (May 30, 2008) http://www.kwwl.com/global/story.asp?s=8400602
[66] C.S. Lewis, *Surprised by Joy: The Shape of my Early Life* (New York: A Harvest Book, Harcourt Inc., 1955), 223.
[67] Ibid, 227.
[68] Ibid, 228.
[69] Ibid, 227.
[70] C.S. Lewis, *The Chronicles of Narnia* (New York: HarperCollins Publishers, 2001), 538.
[71] Sherwood Eliot Wirt, "The Final Interview of C.S. Lewis," interview by Sherwood Eliot Wirt, Assist News Service, May 7, 1963, http://www.cbn.com/special/Narnia/articles/ans_LewisLastInterviewB.aspx (accessed April 25, 2008).
[72] C.S. Lewis, *The Chronicles of Narnia* (New York: HarperCollins Publishers, 2001), 518.
[73] Walter Hooper, "Oxford's Bonny Fighter," in *C. S. Lewis at the Breakfast Table and Other Reminiscences*, ed. James T. Como, 137-185 (New York: Macmillan Publishing Co., Inc., 1979), 167.
[74] Ibid, 171.
[75] C.S. Lewis, *The Chronicles of Narnia* (New York: HarperCollins Publishers, 2001), 518.
[76] Walter Hooper, "Oxford's Bonny Fighter," in *C. S. Lewis at the Breakfast Table and Other Reminiscences*, ed. James T. Como, 137-185 (New York: Macmillan Publishing Co., Inc., 1979), 156.
[77] Society of the Little Flower, "St. Thérèse 'The Little Flower,'" http://www.littleflower.org/ (accessed June 4, 2008).
[78] "Centenary of St. Thérèse," http://www.ewtn.com/Thérèse/Thérèse.htm (accessed June 4, 2008).
[79] Society of the Little Flower, "St. Thérèse 'The Little Flower,'" http://www.littleflower.org/ (accessed June 4, 2008).
[80] Ibid.
[81] C.S. Lewis, The Chronicles of Narnia (New York: HarperCollins Publishers, 2001), 539.
[82] C.S. Lewis, "God in the Dock," ed. Walter Hooper in The Timeless Writings of C.S. Lewis, 297–532 (New York: Inspirational Press, 1996), 333.
[83] Ibid.
[84] Ibid.
[85] Ibid.
[86] Sherwood Eliot Wirt, "C. S. Lewis on Heaven, Earth, and Outer Space," interview by Sherwood Eliot Wirt, Assist News Service, May 7, 1963,

http://www.cbn.com/special/Narnia/articles/ans_LewisLastInterviewB.aspx (accessed April 25, 2008).
[87] "Iowa National Guard unit deploys to Iraq," KWWL.com (June 5, 2008) http://www.kwwl.com/global/story.asp?s=8439691
[88] Ibid.

SECTION TWO

[1] C.S. Lewis, *Christian Behaviour* (New York: The Macmillan Company, 1944), 10.
[2] C.S. Lewis, *The Chronicles of Narnia* (New York: HarperCollins Publishers, 2001), 432.
[3] Ibid, 434.
[4] Ibid.
[5] Ibid.
[6] Ibid, 436.
[7] Ibid, 457.
[8] C.S. Lewis, *Christian Behaviour* (New York: The Macmillan Company, 1944), 9.
[9] Graeme Paton, "Intelligent People 'less likely to believe in God'," *Telegraph.co.uk* (June 13, 2008), accessed June 23, 2008
http://www.telegraph.co.uk/news/uknews/2111174/Intelligent-people-'less-likely-to-believe-in-God'.html
[10] Ibid.
[11] Ibid.
[12] C.S. Lewis, *Christian Behaviour* (New York: The Macmillan Company, 1944), 9.
[13] Ibid, 13.
[14] Ibid.
[15] C.S. Lewis, *The Chronicles of Narnia* (New York: HarperCollins Publishers, 2001), 466.
[16] Ibid.
[17] Ibid.
[18] C.S. Lewis, *Surprised by Joy: The Shape of my Early Life* (New York: A Harvest Book, Harcourt Inc., 1955), 103.
[19] Ibid, 108.
[20] Ibid, 109.
[21] C.S. Lewis, *The Chronicles of Narnia* (New York: HarperCollins Publishers, 2001), 474.
[22] Ibid, 475.
[23] Ibid.
[24] Ibid.

[25] C.S. Lewis, *Surprised by Joy: The Shape of my Early Life* (New York: A Harvest Book, Harcourt Inc., 1955), 221.
[26] Ibid.
[27] Ibid, 224.
[28] Ibid, 225.
[29] Ibid, 229.
[30] C.S. Lewis, *Christian Behaviour* (New York: The Macmillan Company, 1944), 44.
[31] Ibid, 45.
[32] Ibid.
[33] Ibid.
[34] C.S. Lewis, *The Chronicles of Narnia* (New York: HarperCollins Publishers, 2001), 498.
[35] Bowman, Mary, "A Darker Ignorance: C.S. Lewis and the Nature of the Fall," *Mythlore*, (Summer 2003), http://findarticles.com/p/articles/mi_m0OON/is_1_24/ai_107896947
[36] C.S. Lewis, *The Chronicles of Narnia* (New York: HarperCollins Publishers, 2001), 498.
[37] Ibid, 541.
[38] C.S. Lewis, *Christian Behaviour* (New York: The Macmillan Company, 1944), 47.
[39] Ibid, 49.
[40] Ibid.
[41] Ibid.
[42] Ibid, 47.
[43] Ibid.
[44] Ibid.
[45] Ibid, 49.
[46] C.S. Lewis, *The Chronicles of Narnia* (New York: HarperCollins Publishers, 2001), 522.
[47] Ibid.
[48] W.H. Lewis, ed., *Letters of C.S. Lewis* (London: The Chaucer Press, 1966), 21.
[49] Ibid, 22.
[50] Ibid, 21.
[51] Ibid.
[52] Ibid.
[53] Ibid.
[54] Douglas Gresham, "The Man Behind Narnia," interview by Craig von Bushek, CBN.com, http://www.cbn.com/media/index.aspx?s=/cbncom/current/studio10/DougGreshIntvPt1&prgm=studio10 (accessed July 17, 2008).

55 C.S. Lewis, *Christian Behaviour* (New York: The Macmillan Company, 1944), 53.
56 Ibid.
57 EWTN, "Mother Teresa of Calcutta: Peacemaker, Pioneer, Legend," http://www.ewtn.com/motherteresa/ (accessed July 17, 2008).
58 Ibid.
59 Ibid.
60 Ibid.

SECTION THREE

1 C.S. Lewis, *Christian Behaviour* (New York: The Macmillan Company, 1944), 60.
2 C.S. Lewis, *The Chronicles of Narnia* (New York: HarperCollins Publishers, 2001), 490.
3 Ibid, 491.
4 C.S. Lewis, *Christian Behaviour* (New York: The Macmillan Company, 1944), 60.
5 Ibid.
6 Ibid.
7 C.S. Lewis, *The Chronicles of Narnia* (New York: HarperCollins Publishers, 2001), 491. 8 Ibid, 491.
9 C.S. Lewis, *Christian Behaviour* (New York: The Macmillan Company, 1944), 61.
10 Stephen R. Covey, A. Roger Merrill, & Rebecca R. Merrill, *First Things First* (New York: Free Press, 2003), 66.
11 Ibid.
12 Ibid.
13 Ibid.
14 Ibid.
15 Ibid.
16 Ibid.
17 Ibid.
18 Ibid, 67.
19 Ibid, 68.
20 Viktor E. Frankl, Man's Search for Meaning (Pocket Books: New York, 1984), 98.
21 Ibid, 99.
22 C.S. Lewis, *The Chronicles of Narnia* (New York: HarperCollins Publishers, 2001), 484.
23 Ibid.

[24] Ibid.
[25] Laurence Harwood, *C. S. Lewis, My Godfather* (Downers Grove, IL: InterVarsity Press, 2007), 124.
[26] Ibid.
[27] Ibid.
[28] Ibid.
[29] Ibid.
[30] Ibid, 124-25.
[31] Ibid, 125.
[32] Ibid, 124.
[33] C.S. Lewis, *Christian Behaviour* (New York: The Macmillan Company, 1944), 10.
[34] C.S. Lewis, *The Chronicles of Narnia* (New York: HarperCollins Publishers, 2001), 476.
[35] Ibid, 478.
[36] Ibid, 479.
[37] C.S. Lewis, *Christian Behaviour* (New York: The Macmillan Company, 1944), 45.
[38] C. S. Lewis, *The Chronicles of Narnia* (New York: HarperCollins Publishers, 2001), 479.
[39] C. S. Lewis, *Christian Behaviour* (New York: The Macmillan Company, 1944), 47-48.
[40] C. S. Lewis, *The Chronicles of Narnia* (New York: HarperCollins Publishers, 2001), 506.
[41] Ibid.
[42] Ibid.
[43] Ibid, 507.
[44] Ibid.
[45] Ibid.
[46] Ibid.
[47] Ibid.
[48] Ibid.
[49] Ibid.
[50] Ibid.
[51] Ibid.
[52] Ibid.
[53] Ibid.
[54] Ibid.
[54] Ibid.
[55] Ibid.
[56] Ibid.
[57] Ibid.

58 Ibid.
59 Ibid.
60 C. S. Lewis, *Christian Behaviour* (New York: The Macmillan Company, 1944), 61.
61 Ibid.
62 Ibid.
63 Ibid.
64 Ibid, 62.
65 Ibid.
66 Ibid.
67 Ibid.
68 Ibid.
69 Ibid.
70 Ibid, 64.
71 http://www.emmitsburg.net/setonshrine/
72 Ibid.
73 C. S. Lewis, The Timeless Writings of C.S. Lewis: Pilgrim's Regress, Christian Reflections, God in the Dock (New York: Inspirational Press, 1996), 311.
74 Ibid.
75 Ibid.
76 Ibid, 312.
77 C. S. Lewis, *The Chronicles of Narnia* (New York: HarperCollins Publishers, 2001), 457.
78 Ibid, 458.
79 Ibid, 478.
80 C.S. Lewis, *Surprised by Joy: The Shape of my Early Life* (New York: A Harvest Book, Harcourt Inc., 1955), 199.
81 Ibid.
82 Ibid, 200.
83 Ibid.
84 Ibid.
85 Ibid.
86 Ibid.
87 C. S. Lewis, *The Chronicles of Narnia* (New York: HarperCollins Publishers, 2001), 530.
88 W.H. Lewis, ed., *Letters of C.S. Lewis* (London: The Chaucer Press, 1966), 148.
89 Ibid.
90 C. S. Lewis, *Christian Behaviour* (New York: The Macmillan Company, 1944), 69.
91 Ibid.

92 Ibid, 70.
93 C. S. Lewis, *The Chronicles of Narnia* (New York: HarperCollins Publishers, 2001), 530.
94 Ibid.
95 Ibid.

Section Four

1 C.S. Lewis, *Christian Behaviour* (New York: The Macmillan Company, 1944), 10.
2 C.S. Lewis, *The Chronicles of Narnia* (New York: HarperCollins Publishers, 2001), 450.
3 Ibid.
4 Ibid.
5 Ibid.
6 Ibid.
7 C.S. Lewis, *Christian Behaviour* (New York: The Macmillan Company, 1944), 10.
8 Ibid, 11.
9 Harriet Beecher Stowe Center, *Harriet Beecher Stowe's Life and Times* (accessed February 17, 2009), http://www.harrietbeecherstowe.org/life/#uncle
10 C.S. Lewis, *The Chronicles of Narnia* (New York: HarperCollins Publishers, 2001), 434.
11 Ibid.
12 Ibid.
13 Ibid.
14 C.S. Lewis, *Christian Behaviour* (New York: The Macmillan Company, 1944), 17.
15 Ibid.
16 Ibid.
17 Ibid.
18 Ibid.
19 W.H. Lewis, ed., *Letters of C.S. Lewis* (London: The Chaucer Press, 1966), 20.
20 Ibid.
21 Ibid, 21.
22 C.S. Lewis, *The Chronicles of Narnia* (New York: HarperCollins Publishers, 2001), 475.
23 Ibid.
24 C.S. Lewis, *Christian Behaviour* (New York: The Macmillan Company, 1944), 40.
25 Ibid.

[26] C.S. Lewis, *The Chronicles of Narnia* (New York: HarperCollins Publishers, 2001), 476.
[27] The I Have a Dream Speech, U.S. Constitution Online (accessed February 24, 2009), http://www.usconstitution.net/dream.html
[28] Ibid.
[29] C.S. Lewis, *Christian Behaviour* (New York: The Macmillan Company, 1944), 41.
[30] C.S. Lewis, *Beyond Personality* (New York: The Macmillan Company, 1945), 67.
[31] Ibid, 66.
[32] Ibid, 68.
[33] Saint Francis of Assisi, *Catholic Online* (accessed February 25, 2009), http://www.catholic.org/saints/saint.php?saint_id=50
[34] C.S. Lewis, *The Chronicles of Narnia* (New York: HarperCollins Publishers, 2001), 537.
[35] Ibid.
[36] Ibid.
[37] Ibid.
[38] Ibid.
[39] Ibid, 538.
[40] C.S. Lewis, *Chrisitian Reflections* (Grand Rapids, Michigan: William B. Eerdmans Publishing Company, 1967), 81.
[41] Ibid.
[42] Ibid, 80.
[43] Ibid, 77.
[44] Stephen R. Covey, A. Roger Merrill, & Rebecca R. Merrill, *First Things First* (New York: Free Press, 2003), 74.
[45] Ibid, 73.
[46] C.S. Lewis, *The Chronicles of Narnia* (New York: HarperCollins Publishers, 2001), 465.
[47] Ibid.
[48] C.S. Lewis, *Beyond Personality* (New York: The Macmillan Company, 1945), 33.
[49] Ibid, 36.
[50] Ibid, 34.
[51] Ibid.
[52] C.S. Lewis, *The Chronicles of Narnia* (New York: HarperCollins Publishers, 2001), 507.
[53] Ibid.
[54] C.S. Lewis, *Beyond Personality* (New York: The Macmillan Company, 1945), 39.
[55] Ibid, 37.

[56] Ibid.
[57] Kathy Crockett, Lifesaver Hero: Paul Rusesabinga, *The My Hero Project* (accessed March 5, 2009), http://www.myhero.com/myhero/hero.asp?hero=Paul_Rusesabagina_06
[58] C.S. Lewis, *Beyond Personality* (New York: The Macmillan Company, 1945), 36.

Bibliography

Associated Press, "Iowa tornado rated state's strongest in 32 years," (May 28, 2008) http://ap.google.com/article/ALeqM5iMxAxJ-Orfj5UrRL2NjxzG_4-TrAD90U8B5O0

Bailey, George. "Chapter Four: In the University," in *C. S. Lewis Speaker and Teacher,* ed. Carolyn Keefe, 79-92 (Grand Rapids Michigan: Zondervan Publishing House, 1971.

Bowman, Mary. "A Darker Ignorance: C.S. Lewis and the Nature of the Fall," *Mythlore,* (Summer 2003), http://findarticles.com/p/articles/mi_m0OON/is_1_24/ai_107896947

"Centenary of St. Thérèse," http://www.ewtn.com/Thérèse/Thérèse.htm (accessed June 4, 2008).

Covey, Stephen R., Merrill, A. Roger & Rebecca R. Merrill, *First Things First.* New York: Free Press, 2003.

Kathy Crockett, Lifesaver Hero: Paul Rusesabinga, *The My Hero Project* (accessed March 5, 2009), http://www.myhero.com/myhero/hero.asp?hero=Paul_Rusesabagina_06

Dorsett, Lyle W. and Marjorie Lamp Meads, eds. *C.S. Lewis Letters to Children.* New York: Macmillan Publishing Company, 1985.

Elizabeth Anne Seton, Emmitsburg Area Historical Society, (accessed January 31, 2009) http://www.emmitsburg.net/setonshrine/

EWTN, "Mother Teresa of Calcutta: Peacemaker, Pioneer, Legend," http://www.ewtn.com/motherteresa/ (accessed July 17, 2008).

Frankl, Viktor E., *Man's Search for Meaning.* New York: Pocket Books, 1984.

Gandhi, Mahatma. *The Story of My Experiments with Truth,* "Acquaintance with Religions, Part 1, Chapter XX," (Nalanda Digital Library), May 23, 2008,

http://www.nalanda.nitc.ac.in/resources/english/etext-project/biography/gandhi/

Gandhian Institution Bombay Sorvodaya Ma, "Chronology," *A Comprehensive Site,* May 22, 2008, http://www.mkgandhi-sarvodaya.org/under.htm.

Great Lives Great Deeds. Pleasantville, New York: The Reader's Digest Association, 1964.

Green, Roger Lancelyn. "In the Evening," in *C. S. Lewis at the Breakfast Table and Other Reminiscences,* ed. James T. Como, 210-214 (New York: Macmillan Publishing Co., Inc., 1979),

Gresham, Douglas. "The Man Behind Narnia," interview by Craig von Bushek, CBN.com, http://www.cbn.com/media/index.aspx?s=/cbncom/current/studio10/DougGreshIntvPt1&prgm=studio10 (accessed July 17, 2008).

Harriet Beecher Stowe Center, *Harriet Beecher Stowe's Life and Times* (accessed February 17, 2009), http://www.harrietbeecherstowe.org/life/#uncle

Harwood, Laurence. *C. S. Lewis, My Godfather.* Downers Grove, IL: InterVarsity Press, 2007.

Hooper, Walter. "Oxford's Bonny Fighter," in *C. S. Lewis at the Breakfast Table and Other Reminiscences,* ed. James T. Como, 137-185. New York: Macmillan Publishing Co., Inc., 1979.

"Iowa National Guard unit deploys to Iraq," KWWL.com (June 5, 2008) http://www.kwwl.com/global/story.asp?s=8439691

———.ed. *They Stand Together: The Letters of C.S. Lewis to Arthur Greeves (1914-1963).* New York: Macmillan Publishing Company, 1979.

Keller, Helen. *The Story of My Life.* New York: Signet Classics, 2002.

Lewis, C.S. *The Chronicles of Narnia.* New York: HarperCollins Publishers, 2001.

———.*Christian Reflections.* Grand Rapids, Michigan: William B. Eerdmans Publishing Company, 1967.

———.*Christian Behaviour.* New York: The Macmillan Company, 1944).

———.*Beyond Personality.* New York: The Macmillan Company, 1945.

———.*The Timeless Writings of C.S. Lewis: Pilgrim's Regress, Christian Reflections, God in the Dock.* New York: Inspirational Press, 1996.

———.*Surprised by Joy: The Shape of my Early Life.* New York: A Harvest Book, Harcourt Inc., 1955.

———.*Mere Christianity*. New York: The MacMillan Company, 1955.

Lewis, W.H. *Letters of C.S. Lewis*. London: The Chaucer Press, 1966.

Paton, Graeme. "Intelligent People 'less likely to believe in God'," *Telegraph.co.uk* (June 13, 2008), accessed June 23, 2008

Parker-Pope, Tara. "A Hint of Hope as Obesity Rates Hit Plateau," *New York Times* (May 28, 2008),

http://www.nytimes.com/2008/05/28/health/research/28obesity.html?_r=1&th&emc=th&oref=slogin

"Salvation Army's Tornado Relief Efforts," KWWL.com (May 30, 2008) http://www.kwwl.com/global/story.asp?s=8400441

Society of the Little Flower, "St. Thérèse 'The Little Flower,'" http://www.littleflower.org/ (accessed June 4, 2008).

Schulte, Grant. "Iowans Pick Through Tornado Disaster Area," *USA Today* (May 28, 2008)

http://www.usatoday.com/weather/storms/2008-05-27-iowa_tornado_loss_N.htm?csp=34

"Tornadoes of 2008: Neighbors Helping Neighbors - you did an incredible job!," KWWL.com (May 30, 2008) http://www.kwwl.com/Global/category.asp?C=128859&nav=menu82_1

"USDA Rural Development Offers Housing to Tornado Survivors," KWWL.com (May 30, 2008) http://www.kwwl.com/global/story.asp?s=8400602

Wirt, Sherwood Eliot. "C. S. Lewis on Heaven, Earth, and Outer Space," interview by Sherwood Eliot Wirt, Assist News Service, May 7, 1963, http://www.cbn.com/special/Narnia/articles/ans_LewisLastInterviewB.aspx (accessed April 25, 2008).

www.ingramcontent.com/pod-product-compliance
Lightning Source LLC
Chambersburg PA
CBHW062221080426
42734CB00010B/1975